The Age of Inheritance

The Activation of the 13 Chakras

by Sherry Anshara

QuantumPathic™

QUANTUMPATHIC PRESS℠

 Printed in the U.S.A. Published by QuantumPathic Press[sm], 6701 E. Clinton Street, Scottsdale, Arizona 85254 U.S.A. You can contact the author at quantumpathic@cox.net.

Second Edition

Publisher's Cataloging-in-Publication
(Provided by Quality Books, Inc.)

Anshara, Sherry.
The age of inheritance : the activation of the 13 chakras / by Sherry Anshara.
p. cm.
ISBN 0-9742144-0-X
1. Chakras--Miscellanea. 2. Mental healing.
I. Title.
BF1442.C53A34 2004 131.22
QBI33-1794

Book and Cover design by Estudio Ray
Illustration by Joe Ray

Acknowledgements

I would like to acknowledge the following individuals who inspired me, gave of their valuable time, or assisted me in some way during the process of "living" this book and its message. It is with overwhelming gratitude, gratefulness and thankfulness that I honor the following: my students, whose lives were transformed and in return touched me in so many ways; Barbara Changas, who provided, in unconditional love, a safe haven to initiate this book; Anmara, who was inspired to channel the colors and crystals used to vibrationally enhance the Thirteen Chakras; Chris and Joe Ray of Estudio Ray, for their creative talents on the cover design and book illustrations; Susan Grapentine for her brilliant editing contributions; Marilyn Crase for transcribing this wondrous message; and most of all, to the Universal Consciousness of Oneness, and to Bashebar Metaphista who showed me the way.

In Love & Light,
Sherry Anshara

Table of Contents

Illustrations

Along My Way

Prior to 1991, if anyone had asked me if I thought I would be doing what I am doing today, I would have told them, "You're crazy!"

The funny thing is, I always knew I wanted to write a book. I did not envision writing a book like this one. Since I now comprehend that nothing is ever what we think it is, my life is definitely not at all what I thought it would be.

Looking back, I had many unusual episodes and experiences that did not fit the 'norm' at the time. As a very young child I saw lights emanating from people and sometimes around objects. Sometimes it appeared to me as if I was watching a movie. I could see objects, symbols, and colors in the light surrounding a person. But I realized very early that talking about any of this was not appropriate. This frustrated me as a child.

The paranormal was never discussed in my family, certainly not with me. The concept of precognition was not even a consideration to be discussed; yet, I had many experiences of knowing something would happen before it did.

In one incident, what my mother called, "a scary moment", I had one of those "feelings." At age nine my mother and I, vacationing with my aunt and uncle, were staying at a cottage on a lake in the Upper Peninsula of Michigan. It was a fairly remote area.

My mother and aunt wanted to row across the lake to spend time together alone to talk as girlfriends. As a rule I was an independent child, not minding when my mother left. On this particular day, however, I had an intense feeling that danger threatened them if they went out on the lake alone.

My feelings were so clear, I threw a temper tantrum to stop them from going. At the time I was unable to articulate my intuitive feelings. My mother, angered by my unusual behavior, was embarrassed. My aunt was also taken aback by my tantrum. In order to pacify me, they begrudgingly took me along, but they were aggravated at not being able to be alone.

Together we rowed across the lake to a little marshy island. When we arrived they got out to walk around, leaving me in the boat. Within minutes they were up to their knees in quicksand. They screamed, and I screamed with them. I was terrified. I knew what I had felt earlier was now happening. Fortunately for all of us, my uncle heard us. Jumping into a motorboat, he came to our rescue.

My mother was uncomfortable with these kinds of events. She didn't understand my precognizant abilities. She wished that I would not "do them" and not talk about them. What neither she nor I understood at the time was that they just happened. I wasn't doing anything.

Deep, deep inside of me, I always felt connected to something beyond the here and now. Yet I learned not to talk about it to anyone. I did not want to be considered weird. Throughout my entire life, I had many pre-cognitive experiences. Some seemed sad or joyful, but to me it was merely information. My idea was to control it and not expose myself to the world.

I was a young woman in the sixties when many young people were using drugs. They would talk about their experiences while under the influence, relating stories of visions or their trips. It seemed ridiculous to me to have to use drugs to have out-of-body experiences when I was having them sober and under control. The funniest part of it to me was my closest friends would try to get me drunk so I would "spill the beans". They wanted to know about their futures, their past lives, present day concerns. After two glasses of wine my guard dropped, and I would tell them everything they wanted to know. When it was about the future, it happened just as I told them.

At that time, I was unable to give it a name. The information came readily. I knew what I was doing, but I denied that I was doing it. I did not want to be identified with those weird people we call psychics, intuitives, or, heaven forbid, fortune-tellers.

There are no accidents in life. At twenty-two, I was in an extraordinary auto accident. In a brand new 1965 red Corvette, a block from home when I was hit twice by a Chevy. The Chevy broadsided me, spun around, and hit me again pushing my Corvette over a curb. My car knocked down a 40′ evergreen tree sheering it off at the ground. The force pushed my car into a cement block wall, caving in the front up to the windshield. The crash caused a severe head injury and internal bleeding.

The crash totaled the car and almost totaled me. It was a miracle I lived. I remember being out-of-body, and feeling light and free. I remember the moment I re-entered my physical body. I know now that this was a Near-Death Experience (NDE), but I did not know what to call it at the time. In 1965, I had no intention of telling anyone about it. There was no one I could talk to. Not my husband, my family, my friends - no one would understand. Inside, I felt even more different than before.

So I told no one. I intended to get on with my life. I would do what I thought I was supposed to do: be a wife, work, live the American dream. Even in 1965, my desire was to be a career woman. I wanted to emulate my brothers who were in business. Getting married was not my idea, but I did so because it was part of the program. I called this my "double life", the life I performed on the outside, and the life I experienced within myself. They conflicted.

Life progressed. To a casual observer, even to my family and friends, my life appeared normal. My husband and I had a beautiful home in Michigan. We both drove expensive cars. I was in business. We owned an airplane. We lived the dream, according to the programs of contemporary society. It was a very third dimensional life.

As a businesswoman, I owned businesses, as well as being an executive in a large corporation. I belonged to many professional organizations, such as International Association of Women Pilots,

National Association of Female Executives, Special Interest Video Association, just to name a few. By third dimensional standards my life appeared normal. Sometimes it was normal. Sometimes I loved my life. I had fun. I worked hard and played hard.

Inside me, though, I knew there was more. Not being able to put my finger on what "more" meant, I remained unable to identify what was happening to me. The idea of multiple dimensional experiences had never been part of my reality, even though I had continuously experienced a variety of mysterious phenomena. Then I could not name it – or explain it. Today, this phenomena can be identified as channeling, astral-projection, out-of-body experiences, extra-terrestrial visitations, angelic visitations, precognition, telepathy, empathic moments. All of these experiences were happening to me. Sometimes it was like watching a movie. I was in the movie and in the audience at the same time.

From 1965 to 1991, by all intents and purposes, it appeared to the outside world that I lived an ordinary life. However, life is not always what it seems. For these twenty-six years I still led my double life. My not-normal experiences remained secret. Sometimes in a moment of fun and playfulness, I might reveal information to a friend or client in a style that cloaked the profoundness of the information and how it was coming to me. For example, I might be talking to a friend about her life concerns. In the course of the conversation, I would express caring and concern in a consultative style. My friend had no idea that the source of the information I was relaying originated from an angel, a departed loved one, or spirit guide that I could actually see and hear at that moment.

There are no accidents in life. Twenty-six years later, in 1991, I experienced a car accident even more extraordinary than the one before. A foreshadowing of this accident came to me a month before while I was under hypnosis for a past-life regression. Feeling as if I was in a very dark, oppressive place, I felt terrified. Panicked, I forced myself out of the hypnotic state abruptly, not knowing what this feeling was. I decided I was not going to go there. From this experience, I knew deep inside of me that something awful was going to happen, something that I did not like or want. I just wanted to ignore it. If I did not think about it, it would go away.

A month later an occurrence happened that I have come to define as a "set-up." A "set-up" comes about when the Higher Self overrides the ego for the purpose of placing us in a situation, condition, or a "twist of fate" that changes our lives in a profound way. I was in New York City at a corporate tradeshow attended by approximately 30,000 people. Out of all the people who were there, an acquaintance from high school walked up to my booth and said, "Don't we know each other?"

"Oh, my God, we went to the same high school!" I exclaimed, and asked, "What are the odds of us running into each other here at the Javitz Center?"

We chatted and laughed about school. After a brief conversation she asked me when I would be on the East Coast again. "As a matter of fact, I will be in Boston next month, the week of Memorial Day weekend," I replied.

"What a coincidence, so will my husband and I. When are you flying back to Michigan?" she asked.

"My business conference ends Friday at 5:00. Then I head for the airport," I responded.

She stepped back and said in amazement, "My husband and I are through with our business at 5:00 that same day. So, instead of flying back to Michigan, why don't we just pick you up, and you can come with us to Connecticut and stay with us over the Memorial Day weekend?"

"Sounds like fun." So we made our plan. Little did I know how that plan would change my life.

That particular Friday after 5:00, the three of us drove from Boston to Connecticut. We had dinner and decided to go out for dessert and drinks in a neighboring town. She parked, and we began walking toward the restaurant. While we were walking an acquaintance of hers called her over to say hello. I said I would go on ahead into the restaurant and wait for her there.

As I was walking across the parking lot, a woman in her car was backing out of her parking space and smashed into the car behind her. Then she pulled it forward, back into the parking space. She swung her door open and stumbled out, obviously drunk. She asked me if I could help her get her car out of the parking spot.

As I remember this part of the "set-up" now I ask myself, "What the hell was I thinking?"

With my purse on my shoulder, which contained all my identification, I got into the car. I put her car into reverse. Like a shot, it smashed into the same car behind her again. I could not believe it! I thought to myself, "I'm in big time trouble while I was trying to help someone." After putting the car into neutral, it went from zero to sixty heading for the metal fencing surrounding the parking lot, which overlooked a marina mooring luxury boats and yachts.

Seeing the railing ahead of me, I expected the car to be stopped by the fencing. Instead, the railing served to catapult the car, and me, approximately forty feet in the air. The car flipped over in the air, landing upside down in the water, and settled at the bottom of the Connecticut River. My body was trapped in the upside down car fifteen feet below the surface. But I was not there.

As soon as the car took off, I was out of my body flying through the tunnel. The next thing I knew, I was having an extraordinary conversation with twelve light beings dressed in iridescent white robes. To me they looked tangible, as if they had physical form. We were on what seemed like a space ship hovering over the river just above the accident. I could see people running around, trying to figure out what happened. I watched it in living color but felt very detached from the events happening below. I could not have cared less.

What struck me funny was that the only color in the room was me. That day I wore a black and white knit jacket with red piping, a black skirt, and a matching black and white knit top. Amusingly, the knit top had an embroidered nautical anchor on it. I thought how profound and coincidental.

The red piping on my jacket and the black in the outfit was the only color in the room. Even though I was overwhelmed, I still felt safe. The feeling of unconditional love permeated my being. Love was all around. Unconditional love enveloped me. Not a physical word was spoken. But I knew I had choices to make. I grimaced to myself, "Do they really expect me to get back into that body?" The truth is, it was up to me.

What I was given to know is, it would be more than just me who would be returning to that body, a body that I really did not want anymore. I just wanted to be free and go home. Home was not Earth. What I was given to understand, and the agreement I made at the time, was that thirty-two celestial beings from a variety of dimensions would accompany me.

These beings would be housed in my body with me. My body would facilitate the missions of each one during various times, by allowing them a physical expression of their messages. My body would be the channel for them to fulfill their purpose and our agreement. Their purpose was to communicate messages in the form of poetry, songs, writings, speaking, drawings and intuitive healing. These messages would be designed to help human beings empower themselves.

My visit with these beings radiating this love transformed me. Through unspoken communication, I understood I would be returning to my body. The next thing I knew I was in a tube shooting up from inside the car to the top of the water. When I reached the surface, I opened my eyes to see people on the docks. I had no idea how much time had passed. I had just experienced "No-Time." Time did not exist where I had been. "I can't swim," I screamed at everyone. Someone reached me from behind and lifted me up onto the dock.

As I was lying on the dock, I remembered saying to the people hovering over me that I was going into shock. I tried to get up. Someone said, "Lay still." I replied, "I have to get up and go home." Someone in the crowd asked, "Where do you live?" They laughed when I said, "Michigan."

Still trying to get up, I heard a man's voice telling me to lie still, that I had a head injury. I reached up to touch the gash in my forehead, and blood ran down my arm. The ambulance arrived.

I was whisked to the hospital emergency room. The strange part about that was the emergency room doctor said that I required stitches. For some unknown reason I said to him, "I was told if ever I was in an accident, and required stitches, to ask for a plastic surgeon." He looked at me and said, "I'll get one." I was unsure who inside me orchestrated this situation. Looking through my eyes, everything around me appeared different.

The doctors said they wanted me to stay at the hospital for observation. The next day I was admitted. As a result of the accident, bruisings and swellings began to manifest on my body, particularly my face and head. These outward physical injuries were normal considering the trauma of the accident. However, when I looked in the mirror, I looked different to me from the inside.

I felt different from the inside. When I looked in the mirror, I had no idea who the person in the mirror was. I was changed. Part of me seemed to be me. The rest of me was not me. The rest of me was someone else or a combination of someones whom I did not know. My roommate in the hospital room had a little girl about three years old. When she came to visit her mother, she began to stare at me and told her parents about a light around me. She wanted to get physically close to me to be embraced by that light. Her parents were astounded. This little girl did not want to leave my side. I did not know what to make of this.

Word got around the hospital about this lady who had been involved in an unusual accident. "Good Samaritan" they called me in the local newspapers. The papers reported that I had been trying to help a drunken woman and almost killed myself in the process. Since this was a teaching hospital, doctors making their rounds would come and see me with their residents. Curious about what had happened, they wanted to talk to me about my experience. I was even interviewed by a psychologist and a psychiatrist. Some element in my story that I told over and over piqued their interest. They kept asking me how I got out of the car. I would say, "Do you want me to tell you how I got out? Or how you think I got out?" To me there was a significant difference.

Parts of my experience I could not share with anyone, because it was difficult even for me to accept what had occurred. Who would believe me anyway? Certainly not the doctors or the hospital staff! How could I explain my experience to them without them thinking I was nuts? I chose not to do that to myself. So I gave them the best version I could while trying to put it all together myself.

That first morning when they brought me breakfast, I told them, "I absolutely have to have raw food, nothing cooked." I have no idea where that was coming from. I just knew my body required only raw food. The staff dietician came to see me immediately. She said, "I'm the expert here. We have the best food to make you recover better." I replied, "I insist on eating only raw food, fruits and vegetables. That is all I want to eat." We compromised, cooked oatmeal and the rest was raw. I knew she thought it was ridiculous. The truth was, I agreed with her but some force inside of me said "raw foods only."

I would walk around the hospital in what I could only describe as a euphoric state. In some moments, it was as if I had never seen a hospital before, as something I was experiencing for the first time. As Sherry, I had been in hospitals before. Yet through my new eyes, it seemed as though all of this was new. The sense of curiosity puzzled me. Why should this experience seem so unusual? Who was it that was having this unusual experience? Who was looking through my eyes? It would be quite a while before I found out.

The plastic surgeon visited me three days later. He had come to see my progress and was amazed. My head injury, which he had so skillfully stitched up, was almost completely healed. He reminded me of our first encounter in the emergency room. He said, "When I first saw you, it was as if you were orchestrating the hospital staff on how to take care of you. I found you calm, deliberate in your directions, intelligent, not pushy, but in a matter-of-fact way." I said, laughingly, "If I was so intelligent in my directions, I should have asked for a facelift, too." He got the biggest kick out of that. Maybe someday he will give me a facelift, or a facelift to that person who was so calmly directing my emergency room experience.

Another funny thing happened during my stay. The hospital

operator called me, asking me if I was a celebrity. I didn't know what she was talking about. She said, "We have never had so many phone calls from all over the country asking about a patient." I told her I was just as amazed as she was. Perhaps from the notoriety of the accident, people could not believe I was alive. My pilot friends called me. "Sherry, you are supposed to fly airplanes, not cars." The truth is, I was beginning to fly in a different way.

After a week's stay, I decided it was time to return to Michigan. Although I suffered a traumatic head injury and an incredible Near-Death Experience, I knew it was time to go home, at least to my idea of home. I informed the doctors and staff I was leaving. They gave me painkillers to relieve the pain while traveling, and off I went.

I knew in every part of my being that my life would never, ever be the same as it had been before. Before this incident, I could never have imagined what lay before me in the next ten years. Many times in the years that followed I wondered why I didn't just die. It would have been so much easier. For me, death is a piece of cake. Living is the challenge. I have learned so much about myself, about my agreements with these beings, and yet there is so much more to learn. We are just beginning to scratch the surface of knowing who we really are. Our race is in its infancy, even though our technology is advancing at a rate almost incomprehensible. We, as a people, are not evolving consciously as quickly as our technology. The comparable rate of the two is disproportionate.

The old Fear Programs under which we are still operating can be dangerous to our existence, like a child playing with an atomic bomb. This reminds me of an old *Twilight Zone* program. In this particular story, a little boy had 'the Force' and said in his childish way, "If I don't like something, I can make it go away." Most of the town and its people disappeared. The few people left in that town were terrified. Fear ruled their choices. We have 'the Force' in each of us. For us to live, it is time for us to let go of our fears about each other, each other's religions, gods, ways of thinking and doing, whatever keeps us separate. The only thing created out of fear is destruction and death, over and over, century after century, day after day.

Fear rules. It is time to change the rules.

One of the visions that was given to me was to build a healing center. I could not comprehend it. I know I am not the only person on this planet who has had the same vision. It is a part of the collective consciousness of all of us who are seeking healing within.

After my accident in 1991, I began to have multi-dimensional experiences in multi-faceted ways. Although I tried to live the ordinary life I so desired, it was over. I actually tried to commit suicide three different times between 1991 and 1995. Each time my efforts were thwarted. I cannot express in words the pain, confusion and exhaustion of being here. The more I tried, the harder it got. I thought that I was supposed to do something. I tried to live my life operating under the same old third dimensional ways of thinking and doing, but it was not working. I lost my job. I tried to start another company. I even got contracts, but I simply could not pull anything together. I would be sitting in a business meeting, and suddenly, before my eyes, I saw angelic beings, spiritual guides, departed relatives or extra-terrestrial beings as clearly as I could see the meeting participants. I found myself having conversations with them. The next thing I knew, everyone would be staring at me.

These beings were unseen by everyone else. In the middle of the meeting, for instance, someone's grandfather would appear, tell me his name and give me a message for a particular person in the room. Still in the middle of the meeting, I would describe the grandfather, give his name, and pass on the message. It would cause chaos. This was not fun for me. I found it to be uncontrollable.

It hurt my business credibility to the point of losing my job. Eventually, I lost my house. Most importantly, I lost the direction of the life that I had planned for myself. These multiple dimensional experiences increased, intensified and took over my life.

I discovered that I had a relationship with many non-physical beings that would come and go throughout the next ten years. I had no idea what was in store for me. What I came to rediscover is that during my visit with the twelve iridescent white beings, I had agreed to allow my body to be utilized as a vehicle for the delivery of messages. I sometimes now jokingly call myself a "spiritual receptionist."

One example of my receptionist work was when I was still living in Michigan in the early days after my NDE. I received a message to look in a particular metaphysical publication, *PhenomeNews.* As I was browsing through it, a woman's picture caught my eye. It was an advertisement for a hypnotherapist. I was told to telephone her. Very reluctantly I called her, introduced myself and said I was sorry to bother her. I told her, "It sounds crazy, but I have a message for you from your brother." She began to cry hysterically and said, "You don't know what you're saying." In the ensuing conversation, we found ourselves very emotional. "How soon can I see you?" she asked. The following Sunday, she came to my house.

I was desperate to find a red ink pen for my visit with her. I had no clue as to why I needed a red ink pen. After she arrived, we sat and talked, and I began to do automatic writing with the red ink pen. I found myself writing a very personal message to her in this red ink. The source of the message would not sign the message. In the middle of this experience, I went to get my notebook of sketchings. In this book I had many drawings of faces, not just human faces, but also non-human faces. She looked through the book and found a picture of her brother who had died of AIDS five months prior. She was shocked.

She said, "I have a picture of him from his funeral that I carry in my wallet." She pulled it out and showed it to me, saying, "Look, it's him." His name and photo was printed on the funeral notice. She handed it to me, "Here, put it next to the picture you drew." At that moment his message was signed, not with his formal name, but with a nickname that she had called him. The energy surrounding us was of unconditional love. We both cried. Then she told me that red was his favorite color. Every gift he had bought for her was red.

Another dimension to this story unfolded. She continued to look through my sketchings. Lo and behold, she found a drawing of herself, just as she looked now, but dressed in the garb of a past life, in the seventeenth century in Genoa, Italy. She said, "I always knew I lived there in those times. Thank you so much for helping me heal the pain of my brother's death. And thank you for helping me connect with a part of me that I was remembering."

Over the years, I was prompted to draw, to draw faces of people from this dimension and others who I would be meeting along my way. I drew their faces, and then I would meet them. The explanation of why I was drawing these faces came to me in a poem.

Sherry, Sherry, who
The faces she draws,
From the pencil
Comes the expressions
And the identities
Of the faces she draws.
Who are We, we
Are in the faces she draws,
Expressions in the faces
Of the thoughts that
She draws,
From the expressions
Of the We that
She draws
Comes the lessons,
And teachings from
The faces she draws,
From the lessons and
The teachings comes
The conclusions that
She draws
From the thoughts
And faces of the

We she draws,
From the different
Planes and dimensions
Of the faces of the We
She draws
Comes the teachings
From the lessons from
The faces of the We
That she draws
From the experiences
And the feelings from
The faces of the We that
She draws.
So she continues
To draw the faces
Of the We so she
Can draw from
The faces of the
We that she draws.
We love you.
The We
Together We are the
We with you and thee.

In 1997, I moved to Arizona. Within a year of moving there, I met another face I had drawn. The most interesting thing about this face was that this individual is a UFO researcher and an abductee. After I met him, I would receive information about an upcoming sighting. I would telephone him and relay the information. Later, he would call me back and confirm the accuracy of my information. For me, this was validation of my 'ET' connections.

Long before I met Michael, I had been watching a local television program during which two men were being interviewed about their experiences of having been abducted by extra-terrestrials. On the show, these men showed drawings of the beings who had abducted them. Much to my amazement, I had drawn the same beings. I contacted the television station. The two men from the show came to my house to see me. They were experiencing deep anxiety. They looked at the pictures I had drawn and were confounded by the fact that I was not afraid of these beings.

I told them that my experiences were not fearful ones. My experience with the extra-terrestrials had been very positive. For me, my confirmation was exciting. For them, my confirmation irritated and confused them. I had never felt threatened. I was comfortable with my experiences. However, I never told about them in public. I only shared my experiences with trusted friends. My level of comfort, I believe, came from my Near-Death Experience and the fall out from that experience, including my own paradigm shift of consciousness. I have grown to be comfortable with both a physical reality and a non-physical reality. All was real and all was loving. It even came to a point where I was unsure of which reality I lived in and what was "really" real in this third dimension.

Over these past 12 years, I have had experiences too numerous to put into one book. This book is not about these experiences, but about one experience from one individual, whom I have come to refer to as a "walkabout-talkabout."

Because I had agreed to be a vehicle for many individuals to utilize my physical body as a channel, I found the label "walk-in" not entirely applicable. They do not walk in and stay in the sense of a "walk-in" that has taken over someone's body. These individuals come with a message. They come with a message, a lesson for someone or for a group, or to give channeled healing energies to someone who requires it. So I call them the Walkabout-Talkabouts.

One individual in particular is one of my favorite beings. Her name is Bashebar Metaphista. the rest of this book is her message.

A Note On Wordology

Every word that has ever been said to us, and any words we have used in our lifetime, are stored in our bodies. It is called cellular memory, memorization and sounds. Our memory banks begin to store that information while we are developing in the womb.

Consider the idea of all the words you speak on a daily basis. How do these words affect your daily life? How do the words affect the people to whom you are speaking? Since everything is energy or a form of it, your words are energy, and therefore your actions are the physical expressions of the energetics of your words.

Your words are the molecules of your frequency and vibration. Your words are your sounds of consciousness. Your words emit the molecules of your energy and consciousness into the physical reality that you create from within you. There is nothing outside of you that you do not create from within yourself.

From your words, the energy of your actions are then set into motion. If your thoughts or ideas are inappropriate, then your words are propelled into your physical world generated by the energy of these thoughts and ideas. Your days and your lifetime become activated through those inappropriate fields of your energy and consciousness.

The reality of your life becomes unproductive. Your energy is drained. When your thoughts or ideas are activated by appropriate words of consciousness, the energy of your body's action is productive, uplifting and "energized." This is just they way it is.

Each day, millions and millions, and millions of words of consciousness are emitted into the atmosphere of this planet. Although you may not hear every word spoken, your own body remembers the words that are spoken around you, so begin to listen to yourself at your cellular level of consciousness. Your body will reveal so much. Think about how many words you have spoken over your lifetime or how many words have been spoken to you.

You may or may not be aware or understand from what level of consciousness these words become stored in your body; none the less they become and remain embedded in your body, laying unconscious until they are recalled by an experience or situation. At whatever level of consciousness they are recalled, they affect your behavior, reaction or response to life. Your response may be prompted consciously or your reaction may be triggered from your unconsciousness. You may not know why you are being emotional or you may be completely aware of what is happening. It depends upon your level of self-awareness. Every one of the cells of your body is affected by the consciousness of these words, aware or not. Therefore, what you say, what you hear, and how you behave does have a vital impact on your health and your life every day. Your creative process is based upon your consciousness, even when you are unconscious.

As an exercise, begin to write down the words you use when you talk about yourself. Are they positive, affirming? Or, do the words label you as not deserving, or not worthy? Do your words honor you? Because how you label yourself is how you emit the energy of your consciousness. How your energy is expended has a definite correlation to the quality of your life. The words do stick to you, whether you are aware of them or not. Being aware is simply being conscious that what you create in your life through the use of your words will energize or debilitate your life. Give careful consideration to the words that you speak about yourself, to your family, your friends, your associates, your co-workers, and particularly the words you speak to your children.

All times of your experiences and lifetimes are stored in your body. The past, present and future are significant aspects of your cellular memory, memorization and sound. The word "time" when spelled backwards spells "emit." How you emit your energy and the consciousness of your words throughout your lifetime is the manifestation of your creativity. Whether appropriate or not, your words will tell you what you feel and say about yourself. Your words will either empower you or you will give your power away when you are unconscious of yourself. When you begin to become mindful of your words, you can make productive changes in your life. You can change your future. It is up to you. Your life does not have to be the re-enactment of the past inappropriate words of consciousness that you learned and stored in your cellular memory, memorization and sound. You can release them. Your words can make a difference in your life.

Remember, your body holds your memories, your memorizations, and your sounds. Your thoughts, your ideas, your belief systems, your perceptions, as well as your imagination, your aspirations, and your goals are encapsulated within you at your cellular level. So be aware and conscious of what words you allow to be taken in to your body and to be spoken out loud by you. What you create in your life is based upon the words you speak. You are the Creator, the creativity, the creation, the activator, and the manifestation. What you speak, you will manifest. That is just the way it is.

Here's a great exercise to initiate a pro-active change. Change the words "need" and "needy" to "require." Need and needy are words of lack. They are energy draining words. You do require to have the highest and best in your life, and saying that you require something sets the energy into action in very affirming ways. Change the words "want" and "wanty" to "desire." Want is another lack word, and is another very energy-draining word. The word desire simply means "to sire" or "to birth" your requirement into your physical life in a very positive way. And the frosting on the cake is to absolutely, without a doubt, know that you do deserve that which you require and desire in a very positive way. It works. It is the self-empowerment of pro-active doing.

Take the time to emit your energy from new cellular memory,

new cellular action by being diligent, vigilant, and resilient with your words. Self-support your energy and you will create a life of doing, requiring, desiring and deserving through pro-active, self affirming and self-active words. Wordolgy is your Biology.

Introduction

During a meditation on November 23, 1995, Bashebar Metaphista introduced herself to me. She said that she had come to channel through me, to be a part of my awakening of consciousness. "We are all part of the whole," she stated. Then she went on to say, "Those who have not been listening will begin to listen. This is a time of such joy for some and for others a time of anguish. But it is the same; the difference is just the perception. The information that I am sharing is knowledge. Know that a bridge exists between the dimensions, and that there are steps in the preparation to finding one's gate or doorway between the dimensions, especially the walk into the Fourth dimension of the No-Time and No-space."

I am Bashebar Metaphista, of the Annunaki. This is who I am. I am part of you, not separate. In the reading of this information, it is for your discernment for discovering and uncovering your own Truth, that is the key to your Becoming Who You Really Are, and not as the 'programs' have defined you.

All Essences who have channeled, whether they are Archangels, the Masters, the Pleidians, the beings of Sirius, are all parts of each of you, aspects of you. There is not a separation. Any fear issues of any kind, judgment, denial, hate, manipulation, whatever, are all coming to the surface as part of the Becoming.

This is the perfection of the Becoming, the clearing process right from the core, from the cellular and molecular levels. All the dimensions must clear from the "within" of all beings. All energies are being aligned for the Age of Inheritance. We all inherit. No one is not invited, unless you choose not to be invited. No one is omitted from their Inheritance.

All and each of you, light-workers on your own unique paths, are channels to the knowledge that is buried within each of you at your quantum level. All of you are parts of the puzzle and the galactic schematic outline of the universes. Yes, there may be some vying for position, but everyone is entitled to his or her own view of being Galacticized. This is the outrageousness of the Becoming. The certainty is that we are Becoming collectively One Consciousness. How else can WE ALL of the Universes, all of the dimensions, come together?

This is the biggest play of all. The wonderment is that you, individually, will write your own parts, you will pull your own strings; you will create your own story, your own reality. As "trans" formed beings, you will no longer have to exist in the drama of "his" story. Musical, comedy, serious, you choose your reality, birthed from your creative "Feeling Center", your heart and solar plexus.

You are the star! The Earth, the galaxy, the universe, the dimensions, are all within your own Divine Self. There is nothing on the outside, unless you create it. Whatever the reality you desire, from the frequency of unconditional love from your Feeling Center, you can create as frequently as you choose. This is the Becoming of the "going" into the 4th dimension. This is the creative empowerment of the No-Time No-Space. So create outrageous won-

derment, your Heaven on Earth. Be contagious. Be infectious. The No-Time is upon you. Your Divine Will be done. Bashebar Metaphista.

We are not just spiritual beings having a physical experience. We are multidimensional beings having multiple dimensional experiences right here, right now.

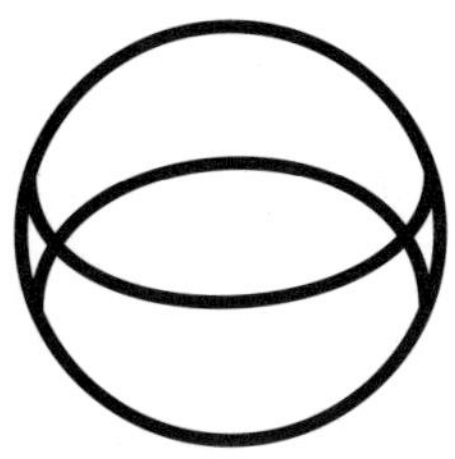

Chapter 1
Your Becoming
The Programming of the Duality Consciousness

Helix Double, not meant this trouble
Helix Double, soon to burst the bubble,
Man Transforms.

Wei Chen
Ancient Poet

The Age of Inheritance, your Becoming, is right here, right now. It is time for everyone to take a stand for themselves individually and collectively to transcend from the old consciousness of all the duality programming, which is based on fear. These fear-based programs have held everyone individually and collectively in a paradigm of opposition. These long-playing programs have reached an end in the evolution of consciousness on this planet.

Over and over again these Duality Programs have interfaced in all of the relationships of cultures and civilizations. The duality consciousness has been the order of the oppositional rules that have governed religions, governments, groups and individuals. It is a fear-based consciousness that must maintain order through control and manipulation. There must always be a judgment or evaluation that insists upon a right and a wrong point of view. That view must include good and evil in the paradigm. Without the judgment from the standpoint of good and evil, the control and manipulation of individuals and groups cannot exist.

The idea of good and evil allows for the space on this planet to hold the energy for an individual or group to control "others." Over the course of history, the rule of authority has changed many times and in many places. The rules of engagement have never changed. The rules of engagement are scripted in the winner being right over the loser being wrong. Taking into consideration that one group may have had more force over another would not be given as the reason why they won. The winner would always invoke that "God" was on their side.

Because Earth is fixed in a linear time of minutes, hours, days, weeks, years, centuries and eons, the evolutionary process of consciousness takes "time." In this process of linear time, the duality consciousness of this Earth is now evolving. The change is coming from within each individual on this planet. The evolution is occurring within the double helix of the DNA that is encoded in everyone. The concept of "so-above so-below" can now be viewed as "so within, so outside." A change is being formulated.

In all of history, the rules said that everything that influenced an individual or group was outside of them. To maintain the outside influence was to continue the order. Looking at consciousness from that point of view, regardless of the history, the governments, the religious orders, or whoever was in charge at the time, the followers were easily ruled, manipulated and controlled through the management of validation. You were not allowed to validate yourself. Validation had to come from outside of you. The odd thing about the Validation Program is that you could always wrong yourself. And, of course, the outside would support you being wrong. The ground rules for the duality consciousness of opposition requires someone to rule, and someone to be ruled. Someone must be right and someone must be wrong. Judgment must always be part of the equation. This is just how "it is" in duality.

The change, occurring at this DNA level, is affecting the entire physical body at the cellular level of consciousness. It is a re-evaluation of consciousness without judgment that is challenging the paradigm of duality at everyone's soul level. Whether you will agree or not, it is happening. This change or transcension of consciousness will not be stopped. For many who find it emotionally and physically too painful to change, will leave this planet through physical death as the move on in their journey. Although it may seem overwhelming and challenging at times, understand that you have agreed to be here. Age, lifestyle or circumstances have nothing to do with it. You agreed to participate in this shift in consciousness. This change is occurring from inside you. You asked to participate. You are a paradigm shifter.

The duality consciousness is embedded in your DNA. It is a double helix. It is not by accident that the number "two" identifies the configuration of the strand of DNA as well as the consciousness experienced through two-sided oppositional forces. What is occurring is a change in the vibrational frequency or resonance of the number two. Your body, this Earth, and the consciousness in which we have co participated and co-existed up to this time are all experiencing this shift in frequency.

Frequency is simply a vibration. In a sense, you can describe frequency as being on the same wave-length (vibration) with someone else or as being part of a group with which you feel compatible (getting along). Not being on the same wave-length with someone or a group is experiencing the vibration from a frequency of opposition. You are out of sync or out of agreement. In the perspective of duality, there is always a right side and wrong side. As the expansion of the frequency from this duality perspective begins to change, you give yourself the opportunity to release a tunnel-vision consciousness. You will then begin to see and experience other views without the frequency of judgment or the perception of right or wrong.

The glue that has held everyone stuck in their version of the Duality Programs is coming unglued. Even the expression of not wanting to be "stuck" in a relationship, in a job, or in a place is being articulated by many on this planet right now. There is a tiredness and exhaustion of living in a vibration of being "stuck." It is not just a matter of looking for a change. It is a matter of feeling that it is time for a change. This feeling is originating from deep inside your body of consciousness. This feeling is a vibration, a feeling that shifts your frequency. It is a rumbling from deep inside of you.

This wave-length of consciousness is expanding and widening

from deep inside your core. For many years it has been called, "The Awakening." It is, indeed, "A Wake" of energy, a consciousness that is beginning to flow throughout the entire physical body. The physical body and all its cells are feeling this wave. It is a physical awakening of the soul, the spirit, and the divine mind. In this Awakening a relationship of these vibrational frequencies is taking place. In the Awakening there is the beginning of an integration of your body, soul, spirit and divine mind. It is a uniting of the Oneness of your consciousness in the physical body on multiple dimensional levels. This Oneness is taking place individual by individual, transforming group by group. It is occurring everywhere. Everyone is being affected. Even in resistance there is acknowledgment that "something is happening."

Oneness is not singularity. Oneness is a unifying field of energy frequencies and consciousness that has been previously separated. The separation of the body, soul, spirit, and divine mind was controlled, manipulated, and maintained because the frequency and vibrational field of the duality consciousness would not allow for this integration. This integration of Oneness simply could not live in this fear frequency.

In duality there is no space or time to hold or maintain the frequency of Oneness. As the frequency and vibrational field expands and unifies, the process of transcension begins. Transcending is shifting from an oppositional force field of fear-laden programs that were encoded in your body, to living in a higher vibrational frequency of unconditional love without judgment.

In this shift there is an exchange in the elements of time from linear to the No-Time/Know Time. This transformation is literally changing form from the inside at the cellular level to creating a new formation of frequency and vibration in which to live. The patterns and behaviors, which were founded on the fear-laden Duality Programs, are so well known.

If there were such a thing as holding on to one fear, it could be the fear of re-creating any version of the old programming by staying in the frequency of duality. Since this planet has not yet experienced a complete shift out of fear, there is so much to look forward to as everyone and this planet transcend to a vibration of unconditional love without judgment. The possibilities, the potentials, are unlimited. Even the idea of disagreement without harm is agreeable.

The Message of this Book is about the programs and the process of moving from a fear frequency of duality and its Seven Chakras to an unlimited fearless consciousness of the Thirteen Chakras. This shift is about initiating a higher consciousness of frequency and vibration from within your physical body for living and creating in a consciousness of unconditional love. Opening and activating the Thirteen Chakras in your physical body, along with the conscious integration of the your body, soul, spirit, and divine mind shifts the duality polarity to a Unison of Frequency and Vibration of Oneness. You are becoming a difference for yourself.

You have a choice to empower yourself and begin your journey of transcension. Buried underneath the layers of the fears and programming, you can now access your divine intelligence and intellect. All this forgotten information is being re-membered from your unconsciousness during this period of the shift. Only you can open the pathways to this information.

You may feel extremely emotional. You may feel more sensitive to your external environment. You may feel more fearful than ever. This is part of the process of releasing the fears that have been embedded in your body of consciousness for lifetimes. Everyday, every week, every year, every decade you have been inundated with information and conversation that reinforces you to live in fear. It is this paradigm from which you are now beginning to transcend.

Every program of fear was designed to immobilize you, to keep you controlled and manipulated individually and as a group. All the formulations of fear were designed to keep you powerless. Although it appeared that when you were part of a group you had power, this was only an illusionary source of power that was always temporary. The intention was to keep you isolated, even when you were part of a group. The illusion of maintaining these tired, worn out Duality Programs is breaking down. There is no empowerment or power in an illusion.

Look around. The old systems are breaking down. The instability is evident. The governments, corporations, and organizations no longer represent a venue of continuity and security. Your own personal sense of security is being challenged. Life in general is appearing more uncertain. All your old ideas and thinking patterns about how you thought it is "supposed" to be are being threatened. Things are simply not the same anymore. They never will be. This wave of change is rippling across the face of this planet from within each individual, radiating from the deepest levels of human consciousness.

In the Duality Programs you will never find balance. Conflict in any and all of its forms, call it what you will - judgment, prejudice, bigotry and so on, never achieves balance with the true nature of life. Duality, by definition, means the conflict between opposing forces or energies. The consciousness of duality is a game of war. The war plays out in relationships, in business, in Corporate America, in religions, between individuals, groups, countries and nations. The scale of the war is measured not by the size, but by the measure of control and manipulation. The persona of the controller is also not gauged by size but by the influence maintained over the manipulated. Whether the controlled is a battered wife, a group, or a nation, it is the fear that allows the manipulation.

War comes in all forms. When you war with yourself, you manifest the participants of the conflict to war with you. When leaders of nations disagree, they enlist their citizens to war with each other. Businesses and corporations do the same. In duality, war is an individual and collective game.

All duality does is continue the game of rulers and subjects, masters and slaves, victimizers and victims, abusers and abused, haves and have-nots, goods and evils, rights and wrongs. These are old, worn out programs, painfully played long enough.

The Dr. Jekell-and-Mr. Hyde syndrome is a perfect example of the duality conflict, representing the perception of good and evil, right and wrong, and heaven and hell. Looking at this concept of reality as an expression of energy instead of a judgment, the internalized energy force becomes the external manifestation whether it expresses itself as good or bad.

The concept of good and evil is an energy of consciousness. It is how the consciousness is propelled through intention that results in the manifestation or behavior of the energy. Inside the human body the conflict is not just internalized by the aspects of good and evil. The conflict of the male and female aspects of consciousness also resides in the human body. This conflict has nothing to do with gender, sexual preference, or sex. It has to do with consciousness and the perceptions of what is masculine and feminine from the standpoint of duality. In duality, it is difficult to conceptualize a unity of the male and female aspects within an individual without thinking of gender. A Oneness of Consciousness is not relevant to gender or duality. Energy in One Consciousness is not separated by opposition.

Everything in the universe is comprised of energy. Energy is the force of vibrational frequencies of consciousness. All frequencies of energy are represented in the Universal Consciousness, whether they are acknowledged or not. Matter vibrates at lower frequencies making it appear solid. When we use physical eyes and yardsticks to measure physical reality, our physical bodies appear solid in our perception. What is unseen by physical eyes and physical measurements still exists, but often remains undetected when using only physical means to provide confirmation.

The soul and the spirit function at a higher frequency of vibration; although, they are housed within the physical body. In the duality consciousness they are separated from each other as though they were outside of the physical body awaiting unity at death.

The body, the spirit, the soul and the divine mind of each human being is One Whole Consciousness and is a series of frequencies much like the octaves in music and sound. The soul, the spirit, and the body of a human being represent a continuum of vibrational frequencies within the make-up of each individual. The continuum includes time, memory, memorization and sound. However, the concept that the soul, spirit, and body is One Continuum and one identity of multiple dimensional experiences, runs counter to the accepted paradigm of duality as a reality in contemporary thought.

The programming of duality is embedded in all the frequencies or levels of consciousness in the physical body. The Duality Programs are energy imprints of consciousness in the DNA and the biology, as well as in the conditioning of the consciousness through language. As explained, Wordology is a huge segment of the energy consciousness of your biology of consciousness.

What we are doing is absorbing granules of energy in the form of words, sounds, language and outside stimuli.

Author?

Chapter 2
The Programs
Judgment, Lack, and Take-Away: The Programs of Fear

The seed of man does not look like a man.
But all the possibilty of Man is contained in it.
History is like that.

Paulos Mar Gregorios
Cosmic Man, The Divine Presence

From childhood on this planet, regardless of the times, you were programmed to give away your power. You were not aware you were doing it. It is through the duality process of being told who you are, what you are expected to be, what group you belong to or what other criteria defines you, that continues to keep you separated from yourself and others. The duality process sets you up for internal conflict right from your beginning. Without consciously being aware of it, little by little, step by step, you give your power away willingly to this false sense of identity. Your behavior then is acted out from and through your duality programming.

As your thoughts continue to be manipulated, you are caught in repeated cycles of behavior, compliments of the duality process. You think you are thinking for yourself, but you are really acting out the behaviors of the conditioning. For millenniums these programs ruled the world. They have ruled your life and your lifetimes.

Why do you think the Reincarnation Programs were invented? On planet Earth the Duality Programs presented a scheme called "karma." How many times have you repeated a program? If this were not the truth, then why are so many individuals throughout the world having past life regressions to understand why they are having repeated issues? These individuals are searching for the reasons, resolutions, and solutions to their karma. Consider the idea of letting go of the concept of karma as either good or bad. Therefore, when you look at karma from a consciousness perspective, how many lifetimes are you willing to invest your energy in learning the same lesson?

Consider an option to find out where these programs are embedded in your body of consciousness and at what level of the unconsciousness, then bring them to your surface awareness, evaluate the information, and make a choice to let the programs go. Or, if you choose to do the lesson again, then by all means, repeat it. It is your choice to continue or cancel your karma. Healing the issues can only come through your choice and your commitment to comprehend your programs and lessons for yourself. Karma is only an assigned label to a consciousness that requires repetition.

Everything that was previously accepted as real and historical is being challenged now. It's about time. It's about the future. And, it's about now. Have you had thoughts about what you have been told is the truth, and what you feel inside is your Truth? Do they feel conflicted? Is there a "duel" going on inside of you? Are your questions feeling more profound? Are you becoming more aware that these questions are coming from a deeper level within you? They are not superficial questions, but emanate from a place to which you had not previously connected in your body. The connection is through "feeling." The feeling germinates the questions from the deeper levels of your awareness, previously unconscious to you. These questions are signaling changes in your consciousness.

The questions are the triggers to accessing the information of memories, memorizations, and sounds that are buried deep within you. This information will reveal the Truth of Who You Are from all of the experiences, the people, and the situations that you have encountered in every journey of your time continuum (past, present, and future). You may even consider, in this time of your journey, your "quest" for your personal holy grail is found within the "quest"-ions and information stored at your cellular level of consciousness.

There are many layers of consciousness throughout your body. In these layers of consciousness there are many versions and personalized adaptations of programming. The programs are all based on fear. It does not matter how you label the expressions of fear, such as anger, frustration, disappointment, worry, bigotry, whichever noun describes the fear, it is still a fear of something. The programs that are discussed in this book are the primary categories under which all the fears of the Duality Programs lay. All the behaviors and actions result from the participation in these programs, whether you are conscious of them or not.

These programs are designed to teach the lessons of the personal and the group journey through the evolution of consciousness. Each individual and each group of individuals, whether they are aware at the time or not, are creating the experiences to learn the lessons, comprehend them, release them or not, and move beyond the fears that pertain to the program. Without conscious awareness, the journey continues through repeated cycles of programs and lessons, regardless of the versions and lifetimes.

The programs and the fears upon which they are based are illusionary. Although they may appear real, they are only an experience of one of the dimensions of consciousness that is within your physical body. Once the fear has been seen as the illusion, fear has no power over anyone. Without power, the emotional attachment to the program disappears.

All of these programs have a commonality in their process. The commonality is the ego. Contrary to popular belief, it is your ego, not God, who judges you as right or wrong. In this role, your ego is your best teacher. Through the programming, your ego will teach you how destructive the force of energy becomes when it is propelled by fear. You will accept this when you are tired of being controlled by fears. Your lessons may have been long and hard in your time continuum, but you eventually will get to your Truth.

At some point in the continuum, you and the groups with whom you participate, through intention and commitment, become willing to override the ego's fear-based indoctrination of the programming by allowing and embracing the return and re-integration of your soul and your spirit within your physical body. As the consciousness of the ego evolves, so does the physical change. By inducing the activation and the integration of the multiple dimensional levels of consciousness within the body, the planet itself begins to change. Through this evolution and integration of consciousness, not only does the energy of the body change, the energy of the Earth shifts into a higher vibration. Because of this shift in consciousness within the body and the Earth, the frequency of the energy and consciousness of the Duality Programs begin to dissipate. Oneness begins to Become.

THE DUALITY PROGRAMS

The Judgment Program

One of the most heinous manifestations of the duality programming is judgment. Judgment is determining that someone else is less than you are. The criteria for judging are unimportant. What is important is that judgment reinforces a belief system that you are separate from each other and one is better. Whenever you or your group judges another individual or group as less, you are giving yourself permission to say you are better than they are. This judging gives rise to mistreatment and separatism. Separatism means you are not only separate, but also reinforces criteria of rank. It is an illusion of power. In this illusion the energy of judgment intends a belief system that this power is true. Hurtful and harmful actions have resulted from the illusional power of judgment.

When observing the dynamics of relationships, whether between individuals or groups, what can be witnessed are the pain and fear of the judged, as well as those doing the judging. Judgment is only based on fear. Fear is based on not having all of the information. Not having all of the information leads to judgment. Judgment is cyclical energy reinforced by fear.

The information that is being presented here is not just from your ego's point of view. But this information is now being presented for all your levels of consciousness, not just from the narrow perspective of the third dimensional reality of duality. All of these levels of consciousness have always been part of your individual journey of your ego, soul and spirit in your physical body throughout all of your lifetimes. However, because of the dense frequency of third dimension, you did not have the ability to access these multiple dimensional levels of consciousness. Now you have both the possibility and the potential to do it. All of this information is found at your cellular level. It is your big picture.

As you go inside in your shift of consciousness, you will find that the Truth about judgment is that you are really judging yourself, be it from this lifetime or your other lifetimes. In the idea of karma, when you have judged others, you will create scenarios at some points in the journey "to be judged" by others. Whatever aspects of the Judgment Program in which you have played, whatever you have not cleared or released from your cellular level, you bring forward into another time.

Underlying the Duality Programs is the foundation of fear upon which the judgment is based. Whatever judgment issue is feared the most, and has not been cleared, will most certainly be relived repeatedly until the judgment issue is resolved within. The debilitating energy of reliving any category of the Judgment Program is not just an individual's repeated karma, but it also affects the dynamics of the karma of a group. The size of the group does not matter. Somewhere along the line, the group of individuals will re-group for the judgment lesson again. In whatever side of the program they participate, be it the judge or the judged, they will re-create the event in the time continuum.

In duality there are always the two sides of the coin. As long as the fear of judgment continues to underwrite the duality programming, there must be those individuals and groups to play in the opposing roles. As long as the Earth is held in a belief system of opposition and judgment, a space is held for the energy of judgment.

Looking at the bigger picture, a space can be created for you as the observer to see the divineness of this Judgment programming. (Divineness does not mean it has to be accepted and continued because everything in the universe is in divine order, good, bad, or indifferent. The divineness is in the lesson learned.) Now in this space of observation, you have the potential to release the illusional fears and the programming. By seeing fears as illusions, you then have the choice to release the energy of opposition and duality from this planet. You do it from within you. As the observer you detach from the fear and the issue without judgment. You get the lesson.

This space of observation cannot be created until all your judgments are released. This is an individual by individual commitment. By allowing your feelings, not your ego's judgment to direct the energy of your consciousness, conscious detachment from the fear of judgment is achievable. Changing your consciousness is only possible through your commitment with intention to detach from the frequency of fear. You can change your frequency and vibration from fear-laden opposition and judgment to Oneness. You make it happen.

A first step in releasing this Duality Program of judgment of a group is to release it individual by individual, because it is each individual within the group that changes the consciousness of the group. As long as one group judges another, fearful opposition will continue. Whatever the Judgment Program is, "my God is better than your God," "my way is better than your way," ask yourself, "Is it really worth the present and future of this planet to continue the Judgment Program?"

Sometimes in the shift of consciousness, it seems chaotic inside. However, there is an order in chaos. The energy of this shift directed with commitment and intention from the inside will change the chaos to order outside.

The order will change the outside dynamics of the thinking, behaviors, and actions of people. As the consciousness of the people change, the space of this planet changes. A new space or dimension not based on the old paradigm (of energy and consciousness) is created and activated. The changes in programming occur from the inside out. It is an inside job. From the core of each individual, the core of the planet's energy shifts. A new dimension manifests for you and the planet and for everyone who chooses to shift.

The Lack Program

The Lack Program is one of duality's most debilitating programs. Lack identifies you as "missing something" or "not having enough of something." It separates you from yourself and from others. It is easy to become "paralyzed" and dysfunctional through the idea of not being enough, not having enough or not being good enough. These paralyzing fears of the Lack Program create a false sense of competition and promote the survival mentality of bigotry, jealousy, envy, distrust, and hatred. The fears within the Lack Program manipulate your thinking patterns, and you manifest cyclical patterns of behavior that reinforce this paradigm.

To support the Lack Program, the underlying personal agenda said that, if you have something, somewhere along your timeline, the "do-not-deserve-it" program would arise. It said, "You are not good enough to have it." So, if by chance you did get it, deep within your unconsciousness, the Lack Program said, "You did not deserve this," or "You are waiting for the ax to fall," or "When will I lose this?" The loss becomes your self-fulfilling prophecy through your behavioral patterns of the Lack Program.

What occurs unconsciously is you prove to yourself and you validate that you didn't deserve "it", i.e. the money, the relationship, the "good thing", whatever the good thing is. The illusion of the Lack Program does not allow for the energy consciousness of "deserving." In the script of the Lack Program, you act it out. You get caught up playing both sides of the drama of having it and then taking it away. The programming runs so deep. You give your power away whether you "have" it or "lose" it. There is no empowerment in lack. Even the idea in duality of abundance is temporary due to the abundance of lack.

Throughout history, even as the ruling powers changed, the manifestations of the Lack Program have remained the same. Though different faces, different places, different times, the dynamics always remain the same. No one ever seemed to have enough. Lack has nothing to do with economics or material acquisitions, including the ownership of land. Lack is a consciousness that holds the energy that there is never enough to go around. Regardless of what it is that "has to go around", the only thing that can be shared in the Lack Program is "lack" itself. This paradigm is founded upon the sharing of the fear principle of "never enough." It is the illusion of sharing the insufficiency. The concept of abundance and prosperity is not compatible with the Lack Program and cannot co-exist in this paradigm. Abundance in duality is based on lack.

In Truth, this planet Earth provides more than enough for everyone. But the fear consciousness of this program is so deeply ingrained in the physical body at the cellular level, that it will take conscious commitment and intention to erase this fear. By recognizing that the lack mentality impacts everyone on this planet, you can choose to exchange this consciousness for a consciousness of abundance and prosperity in which everyone can participate in the real meaning of sharing.

Sharing abundance and prosperity is a higher frequency of consciousness in which lack cannot exist. In sharing from the heart, without the fear of losing, there is abundance and prosperity for everyone. The Earth reflects the energy of our consciousness. In the energy of lack, deficiency rules. The time has come to change the Rule of Lack on this planet.

The hidden agendas the Lack Program embraces are not just scarcity, but sacrifice and disappointment. The theory states that if you work hard enough and long enough and make sacrifices, you will get what you deserve. The issue here is the word, "deserve." In the context of the Lack Program, most of the rewards are temporary or as interpreted by religion, you might get them in the afterlife. Of course, that depends on the Judgment Program.

By some stretch of the imagination, if the reward is manifested by chance in the energy of lack, there seems to be a restriction of time limitations to hold on to the reward. "Things are going so great, it can't last." And, it doesn't. Good things or rewards are difficult to maintain, because of the not-deserving agendas infused into your cellular consciousness from the Lack Program of duality.

This has nothing to do with the idea of being temporary or permanent. Evolution is about change. The difference is that through the process of duality's evolution, the changes are a variety of versions of the same programs, particularly the Lack Program. Although, it may appear that you are evolving from lifetime to lifetime, and the material possessions appear to be bigger and better for a few, the only thing that is really changing is the creativity in which the versions of the Lack Program are scripted.

The versions now just appear to be more sophisticated. The disappointment that occurs from the not-deserving agenda of the Lack Program affects the body physically and can result in serious illness. The disappointment affects your core consciousness on many levels, whether you are aware of it or not. Disappointment is a debilitating emotion. It can be a precursor to depression. It also creates a cycle of consciousness of emotional highs and lows. The peaks are the temporary "highs" to the temporary valleys of the "lows." Lack is a cycle of consciousness that humanity has existed in for lifetimes.

Scarcity is the driving force that perpetuates the control and manipulation of most on this planet. In this paradigm, scarcity is the wedge that maintains separation. Separation, by the fear of not having enough, supports the consciousness that some will be provided for and some will have no provisions. When there is a consciousness of scarcity, there is no room for the consciousness of sharing the wealth.

At the turn of the millennium, Y2K, the fear of scarcity was so great in the U.S. that it manifested into hoarding by many. As ridiculous as it may seem now, the fear of lack overwhelmed the energy of sharing, a perfect example of separatism through lack.

The amazing aspect of humanity's creativity is how many versions, both individually and collectively, there are of the Lack Program. Consider the times in your own life that you felt you had a lack of something. It could have been a variety or combination of lack, i.e. the lack of support of friends and family, lack of enough money, lack of commitment in relationships, lack of material things, lack of abilities, lack of opportunities, lack of self-esteem, lack of self-worth, lack of courage, lack of time, lack of choices, lack of information, even the lack of possibilities. Any version of lack is founded on fears that are ingrained in your physical body of consciousness at your cellular level. They are all versions of the insufficiency consciousness, which has cycled through, not just individuals, but through civilizations time and time again. This false sense of scarcity invented the survival competition.

The Take-Away Program

This false sense of survival competition is dependent upon the duality Take-Away Program. The Take-Away Program expresses itself in the outward appearance of taking away something from another person, a group, or country, and doing it in an impersonal way; although, it is infused with emotions. The Take-Away Program is also expressed through the individual by the not-deserving or punishment format of the program. It is easy to take-away power from someone when they are living life in the fearful consciousness of not-deserving and being unworthy. It is a two-edged blade that cuts very deep.

Embedded in the Take-Away Program is the behavior of taking something away from yourself. As painful as it is to take-away your own power and give it away, it is as debilitating for the individual or group that accepts it from you. Taking away and giving it up are the opposite poles of polarity that hold this consciousness together, but it is the same program. This, too, is temporary. Only a change in consciousness or the death of this consciousness can release it from this planet.

From the group Take-Away Program, only one person or group can rule over others. This established the ruler and the ruled, which formulates the 'haves' and the 'have-nots'. The "haves" gave themselves permission to take from others. Groups used all sorts of excuses, such as divine right, destiny, power, position, having the upper hand, "because my God is better than your God," in the consciousness of the Take-Away Program. They deemed it their right to take-away from others. How much of history, and the information that it provided, was lost through the Take-Away Program?

Consider how the legacies of certain civilizations were destroyed by a version of the Take-Away Program. They were destroyed because of the idea that one group's version of God was better than another's. Consider the actions of a person that demonstrates ownership over another, whether parent/child, husband/wife, master/slave, teacher/student or boss/worker. Ownership is a consciousness of the Take-Away Program. It is based on the fear of lack, and is enacted through the drama of control and manipulation.

It is an energy infused in a paradigm of loss of identity. An individual or group loses their identity through the dynamics of the power exchange. The one that is in the position of the take-away appears to be in the seat of power and gains by taking away. The one that is forced to give up power feels the loss of power through the Take-Away Program. This is the illusion. Regardless of position, both become caught up in a cycle of dependency. A result of dependency, an energy of "wanty-needy" is created. Many relationships are drawn together because of this energy. It is the Law of Dysfunctional Attraction. Most are simply not aware of this consciousness that is emanating from their Generative (sexual) Chakra. This will be discussed later in this book.

Whether this "wanty-needy" consciousness emanates from an individual or a group, this fear-based energy feeds on the reciprocity of dysfunction. The "wanty-needy" aspect of this energy field readily gives up power. The "need-to-be-needed" aspect of this program readily accepts and takes away from the "wanty-needy." There is no real power in this Take-Away Program on either side of the coin. The power is temporary. No satisfaction results in taking away power from another. The take-away behavior stems from the consciousness of lack. Real power is never gained through lack and the Take-Away Programs.

At a time in your journeys, when you were in a "have" program in any lifetime, you "had" to worry about keeping it, and expended your energy by worrying that someone would come along and take "it" away from you. If you lived in your "have-not" lifetime, you struggled through life trying to get what the others had. It was described as your "lot" in life. If it was a lot, then how come it seemed to you that it was not enough? The Lack Program, or the consciousness of not having enough, is the illusion of insufficiency. It is a "lot" of lack.

Each of these three categories supports the energy of separation. The space in this energy holds a frequency and vibration of not only being "separate" but includes the configuration in the consciousness for fragmentation. In fragmentation, aloneness, loneliness, and disconnection are the elements of consciousness that run so deep that sometimes the pain, though illusionary, seems real and overwhelming. Addictions and disassociative disorders become the worse case scenarios.

In these states of consciousness, it appears to be so difficult that the idea of participation in the lesson cannot even be imagined. The ego in this field of consciousness is working from the lowest vibratory frequency of consciousness. The energy of the consciousness is contained in the First Chakra. From the perspective of fear, the energy is so condensed. The concept of evil and darkness is expressed because of this condensation of fear. What is created, then, through the Second Chakra, (the energy of the Generative and Sexual Chakra), connected to the fear-base energy of the First Chakra, are the emotional issues of dysfunctional behaviors and illnesses. This is a consciousness, whether you are aware of it or not. You bring it into the relationships that you attract to you.

Your consciousness, which is also associated with the Seven Basic Chakras, lives within your entire physical body at the cellular level. Each one of your cells and each group of cells, whether an organ or a system, contains all the levels of your consciousness. You are a composite of memory, memorization and sound. You are intelligence and intellect. Underneath the programs and the fears is where you will find the information of all of your experiences and participations in your time continuum. The information is your source and resource to healing the emotional attachments to the programs.

Before you can take back your power and heal, you must be willing to make the commitment to yourself to release the fears of the Judgment, Lack, and Take-Away Programs. In a five-step process to empowerment and healing, the first step is to trust your knowing. Your knowing is that innate sense of certainty you feel at your core. Although you may "know it", there is still no empowerment in just your "knowing." The second step is your understanding. However, there is still no real empowerment in understanding something. Therefore, your creativity and actions can not be changed in the current paradigm of duality. The key to your self empowerment shift in consciousness is the vital third step. It occurs at your cellular level underneath the programming. It is comprehension. When you comprehend something without the dynamics of judgement, lack, and take-away, your life changes because you change it by choice.

As you continue reading, these steps appear to be out of order. They are not. There is a purpose in this order.

1. Knowing

As a child or adult, when someone labeled you as bad or undeserving in some way, inside, at your core, you knew that the label was not your Truth. The label of the judgment, however, became a part of your consciousness. The label affected your actions and behaviors. Because of the judgment, even knowing that this label/judgment is not your Truth, you did not have the power to take a stand for yourself. Knowing is simply not enough, and it cannot empower you. If it did, there would not be so many wounded children within the adult. Knowing is still encased in the energy consciousness of both judgment and lack. Knowing does not have the physical energy to change the consciousness at your core.

2. Understanding

Understanding is the second step in the process. However, the energy of understanding can be ambiguous. Because of the variation in words and language and their meanings, the concept of understanding a meaning can be as varied as the words used to describe it. Many times you "think" you understand something. When the understanding is only from a superficial consciousness, there is no connection to your feeling at your core. When understanding has no feeling, it really is not understanding. It is just perception. Perception has no empowerment. There is no clarity, clarification, or clearing of the emotional attachments to the issues in the energy consciousness of understanding that is based on thinking. Activating your understanding begins when you connect to your knowing through feeling. Understanding releases the dynamics of perception and allows for an energetic pathway conducive to releasing your core consciousness of truthful feelings. Truthful feelings clear the fears. Your pathways to understanding your knowing are open without the fears of the programs.

4. & 5. Creativity and Actions

The fourth and the fifth steps to empowerment and healing yourself are in the energy of your creativity and your actions. In these steps, a change in the paradigm of your consciousness is required. The requirement is to release the fear-based patterns and behaviors that impact your actions. Without clearing your fears, your creativity and your actions are just re-creations and variations of the old programming. Nothing really new is created. Your actions are just different versions of your creativity. The foundation is still the same, based on the Duality Programs of fear. Your knowing is not clear and does not have clarification for your understanding to make real changes to empower and heal yourself. Your creativity and actions cannot change without the third step, comprehension.

3. Comprehension

The third step is your key to empowering and healing yourself to make changes without being fearful. This step is called comprehension. When you comprehend on all levels of your consciousness from your cellular level, you know and understand that you are the Creator and the participant in your life. It is you who participates with everyone, in every situation, in every event, in every lifetime. With comprehension you absolutely know and understand without any doubt that your creativity and resulting behaviors were written and acted out by you alone.

In your consciousness and energy of comprehension, you have no judgment for yourself or others. You have enlightenment and completion with the lessons that you so creatively wrote into your scripts to learn about yourself. In this energy field you become grateful and thankful for all those who participated with you in those situations and events that taught you about yourself.

Comprehension is when the light bulb goes on and you say, "I get it! Not only do I get it, I have it." There is no requirement to rehash the lessons or the programs. It is not necessary to even consider expending your energy on blame, shame, guilt, or any other low-based frequency of the fear consciousness. Comprehension is the key to clearing your fears and issues at the surface consciousness of your physical body. Comprehension is your point of clearing. The change occurs from within. Transcension from the Duality Programs is occurring. You are initiating the release of the programs of Judgment, Lack, and Take-Away. You get it. You have it. You now have nothing to judge yourself about anymore. Since you have it, there is nothing you lack. Regardless of what is going on "outside of you", you are releasing yourself from the fears and the programs. You are consciously empowering and healing yourself. You comprehend that your life is up to you and no one else.

At this point in the consciousness of comprehension, you become the master of your energy and your consciousness. You comprehend that the Judgment, Lack, and Take-Away Programs were the teaching tools for you and your ego to evolve. At this point in your evolution of consciousness, your soul and spirit begin to integrate with your physical body and your ego as Oneness with your divine mind and intellect. You know without doubt or fear. You understand without question. You comprehend your knowing and understanding throughout your body. You feel it.

Your creativity is no longer based on the old patterns of fear. You change your actions. New uncharted creativity becomes your potential and possibilities. In a sense, it is the new birth of a new reality. You take your stand to heal and empower yourself. You will not be drawn back into the old patterns of the dysfunctional laws of attraction, known as the programs of duality.

You know what you know. You understand yourself. You comprehend your life is your creation, and whatever actions you choose, you manifest them. Comprehension frees you from the programs and the fears. Transcension is yours.

Unconscious pain is painful
Until the consciousness of the pain
Is released from your body

Sherry Anshara

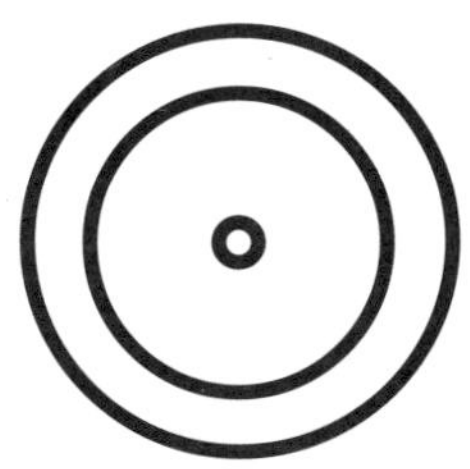

Chapter 3

One Consciousness, Multiple Dimensional

Levels of Consciousness, Programming Versus Awareness

The intention of Man's Being is Life
To the fullest of Man's potentiality.
Man is multifaceted and so is the
Being of One Consciousness-unlimited.
Man is coming out of the illusion-
To Life the Dream.

Sherry Anshara

Consciousness is awareness. Your level of awareness is expressed through the energy of your behavior. Your behavior is exhibited as levels of your awareness or consciousness at the varying points of time in your history. The consciousness of both the collective, and you as the individual, sets the format for the behavior that is exhibited and manifested into your physical world. However, most of the behavior of you as an individual, as well as the collective in which you belong and participate, is exhibited and manifested from the unconscious. Simply, you and most individuals are not aware of why each of you are behaving or acting in a certain way, particularly if it is dysfunctional or destructive. The actions of the behavior are the result of the programming within the physical body. Again, you and most everyone do not realize that everyone has been programmed. The consciousness of the programming is subtle.

The programming is gradual and occurs over a period of time. It is not only embedded in your cellular consciousness over a singular lifetime, but is ingrained in your unconsciousness over lifetimes. Sometimes the programming is deliberate. In the cases of cults, hate groups, and religious zealots, the programming is intentional. Although this type of programming may appear on the surface as having good intentions, it is very destructive to the freedom of you as an individual to think for yourself, as well as controlling and manipulating the group's consciousness, thinking and behavior. The energy and the expression of the energy in this form of indoctrination are only for one purpose, which is always control and manipulation.

Governments have played this game of consciousness manipulation over the centuries. Although there is the illusion that it serves the manipulators to have the ability to control the manipulated, it is always temporary. A rebellion of the consciousness eventually occurs. Because deep within the consciousness of the individual and the group there is a space or place, underneath the programming, that knows this manipulation is not the Truth. It may not be understood or comprehended at the time, but the rebellion will always arise.

The significance of the rise of the rebellion, consciously and metaphorically, is the rising up or ascension of the consciousness. At some point the suppressed become the rebels. Even though it may appear that the rebels lose, the rebellion is a shift in consciousness that has occurred. A paradigm has shifted. At some point from the moment of the rebellion the future is changed. The victory is not always in the outcome of the battle, but in the outcome of the shift in consciousness. Awareness is the result of the shift. Browsing through history, more times than not, the rebels' leaders and, indeed, the followers, become the heroes. Bear in mind that the consciousness of these heroes in later times were still considered the enemy rebels in their own times. The rebellion is the event that brings awareness to the physical dynamics of the consciousness. Inside each individual, the event triggers the questions, "Does this consciousness have value? And does it serve us as individuals or as a group?" Look back through your own life; recall those events where you recognized a shift in your own consciousness. In that shift you realized that a particular consciousness no longer served you and you were no longer willing to participate within the physical and spiritual dynamics of that consciousness. You became the leader of your own rebellion. You were discovering what was right for you, whether you chose to continue in a specific consciousness or not. What you learn is that, indeed, you do have a choice.

Sometimes the most frightening aberration of the control and manipulation programming is the conditioning under the guise of good intentions. This is the control through guilt and blame that is expressed subversively through the illusion of caring. This is a conditioning program of the illusionary "knowing what is best" for someone else.

The dynamics of family behaviors for the purpose of imposing one's idea over the free will of someone else's life and choices is a good example. Even the saying, "I do this because I love you," can result in some of the worst case scenarios of control and manipulation, particularly in an abusee/abuser relationship. Taking this behavior a step further into the dysfunction, many children are controlled through sexual or physical abuse. This consciousness of control and manipulation comes from the lowest-based fear energy of the First Chakra.

The insecurity and powerless consciousness is so dense the Second Chakra can only create and manifest a sickly, dysfunctional behavior of the worst cases of control and manipulation. There is no consciousness or energy of Love in this dense field of fear embedded in the First Chakra, which generates the controlling and manipulative behavior from the Second Chakra.

Each lifetime, for you as an individual and the group or groups in which you participate, has a purpose and a function in the development and the expansion of your consciousness. Overcoming the illusions of the programming, whether it is in your DNA, in your biology, or learned through your conditioning, is what enlightenment is all about for you. Overcoming the programs may appear a complex process; it is not the Truth. The ruse is that you are not smart or strong enough to overcome the programming. Your emotional hooks to the programming bind you so that you can continue to be controlled and manipulated by your fears. Making it appear that something is complex is the perfect scenario to contain your energy and consciousness controlled within the low-based frequency of fear in your First and Second Chakras of the old system. Fear is the consciousness that drives the energy of this old system.

Consciousness on the third dimensional plane produces a behavioral pattern based on what you think you know and based upon your emotions and fears. The awakening is you becoming aware that you are more than who you think you are. The awakening is you becoming aware that there is more to your being and your life than just the physical realm, and that there is much more than what you have been programmed to believe about yourself and the world that you have created.

Transcending the old thought patterns, the old versions of behaviors, the old belief systems is brought about by the expansion of the energy fields of your own consciousness. Everything about you is energy. Every form of your creativity and manifestation of your creativity is an expression of the energy of your consciousness, whether you are aware of it or not. Becoming aware begins your physical and spiritual rise of the consciousness in your physical body.

What happened is that the foundation of your consciousness and the collective consciousness on this planet is based on fear. When you are unaware of any other consciousness or you are unaware that you have other levels of consciousness within your physical body, your behavioral patterns result in repetitious cycles. Not only within this lifetime do these behavioral patterns affect you, but these patterns are also connected to your other lifetimes. These behaviors emerged again and again from the programs that are buried in your unconscious consciousness within your cellular body. This unconscious consciousness drives the energy that recreates the patterns of behavior from within you. It also affects the dynamics of the group behavior in which you participate. There is no judgment in this statement. It is simply the way it is. Your willingness to become aware of all the levels of your unconscious consciousness expands your reality. You become aware of what is best for you. Your behavior changes by choice, not by pain. When the changes begin to occur, sometimes you change groups. (The word "gro-up" means to grow up. Each group in which you participate reflects your growing up process).

Your thoughts are energy. Your thoughts emerge from your consciousness. Your consciousness is energy vibrating at different octaves that produces different levels of awareness. Your awareness, regardless of how dramatically or subtly it occurs, produces an awakening within you. In the time of your Awakening, you will go through a course of events which trigger the expansion process of your consciousness. All of the processes, whether you experience them alone or as a member of a group, are the necessary experiences in which you bring about your own Awakening. In your Awakening process, the integration of your many levels of consciousness begin to connect to each other.

In the divine order of the Awakening, everyone will experience their own unique way through their process of enlightenment. Even from the perspective of time, space, and lifetimes, the process is unique to each individual, as well as to each group. The higher purpose for each of you is to experience in your own unique way your own path to your own enlightenment.

There is no right way or wrong way to experience your Awakening. The actual experiences may differ from individual to individual. What triggers the Awakening process may be a Near-Death Experience, a major loss, a trauma, an illness or some event that changes your perspective about your life and your purposes for being here on Earth. (There is more than one purpose, because you are multiple dimensional).

The purpose of the process is to bring you out of the darkness of fear to the knowledge about yourself, which is the Light. Your knowledge is the Light, which replaces ignorance or your fears. Know ignorance is never bliss. Ignorance is your darkness.

The old paradigm of fear-consciousness and its behaviors no longer serves you or humanity. The time has come to change the fear-consciousness that has ruled over this planet. The objective is for each of you to take back the essence of your life and empower yourself from the core level of consciousness buried underneath the programming of fear. Your expansion of awareness and integration of your multiple dimensional levels of consciousness affect the evolutionary transcension of your DNA, your biology, and your emotional attachments to the programming.

You do this as you develop and create for yourself new practices of thought, speech, and behaviors. The old behavioral games of control and manipulation, more-than-less-than, my God is better than your God or any form or formulation of the Fear Programs will no longer apply. You become aware that what you think and what you say is Who You Are and becomes the creativity and the actions of what you do. Your claim to 'not knowing' also no longer applies to you or your life. Your purposes become on purpose.

You are at a culmination or turning point of releasing the old practices and programs. A point of the Coming Together is occurring from inside of you. Each of you has elected to be here on this planet at this time. The Coming Together is realizing that the answers to all of your questions are inside of you. The source of your empowerment comes from comprehending the information that resides within you. The source of that empowerment is not and has never been outside of you.

Your cellular memory is your database of all the information of Who You Really Are. What is occurring now, at this time, on this planet is that as you awaken to yourself. You realize that you are much more than you have been conditioned to believe about yourself. You are so much more than you can imagine.

The limiting boundaries of the third dimensional fear consciousness restricted your visions and your imagination for yourself. It has been impossible for you or anyone to imagine a concept of being unlimited. Living through the programs of Judgment, Lack, and Take-Away limited everyone's possibilities and potentials. Regardless of acquisitions of material wealth, status, or money, a consciousness of "limit" still prevailed. The programs reinforce limitations.

As you allow yourself or give yourself permission to release the programs, you release the restrictive density of the fear contained in your cellular body. As the physical density of the fear is released, your cellular body has clear open spaces. In these cleared open spaces, there is room for a consciousness that is multiple dimensional and unlimited. The concept of limitation in the word "room" is irrelevant. In third dimensional terms, "room" would imply boundaries. At the cellular level, the clearing of the density is the letting go of the vibration and the frequency of the density of fear. In the transcension of your consciousness, the vibration and frequency of your cells increases. So do the vibration and frequency of your DNA and your biology increase as you release the density of the Fear Programs. In your Higher Consciousness of vibration and frequency, your Unlimited Consciousness becomes the reality. Everything in your life transforms. Imagine that!

In the process of clearing the restricting fear consciousness from your cells, your thoughts, behaviors and actions become clear, and so does who and what you manifest in your life. You have clarity and clarification. In this clarity and clarification, you see the potential and the possibilities for unlimited creativity. Unrestricted, you make new choices in how you participate in life. You are Becoming into the Age of Your Inheritance. You are becoming conscious that you are part of the All, and All is One as a part of You.

Transcending the old thought patterns, the old versions of behaviors, the old belief systems is brought about by the expansion of the energy fields of consciousness. Everything is energy. Every thought, word, and action is an expression of energy. Everything is connected because it is all made up of energy.

In the beginning humans grouped or separated themselves into tribes. These tribes regionalized into states, countries, and nations. Through contemporary commerce everyone has become linked internationally, for example, Nike, McDonald's, the Internet. However, though connected by material product, the consciousness of the separation program once localized has expanded to cover the Earth.

The underlying separation patterns of thought continue to keep people separated from each other. These old thought patterns proliferate the control and manipulation programs under the separatism paradigm, perpetuating the behavior to continue in terms of more-than-less-than, haves-and-have-nots and the controller-and-the controlled.

In this Now time a deeper spiritual rise of consciousness is surfacing on the planet from within each of you. So many of you are beginning to realize that inside yourselves this profound feeling is rising to your own surface consciousness. This feeling is emerging from the Universal Consciousness of Oneness. This Oneness feeling reveals to you that although individuals may appear different, speak a different language, come from a different culture, or have a different version of God, the difference is not different. This feeling is a vibration and a frequency of connectedness. This vibrational frequency holds a resonance of remembrance and familiarity. The familiarity is you remembering that you are connected to the Oneness of yourself and everyone.

As these deepest levels of your frequency and vibration rise to your surface consciousness, you are awakening. This feeling emerges from your personal connection to the Universal Consciousness of Oneness. You are not only recognizing your inter-link to the Universal Consciousness of One, but also realizing that everyone is connected as One to you.

All of you are in the practice time of this paradigm shift. This is occurring not through your emotions, but through the frequency and vibration of feeling. Your feeling is your deeper level of communication that transcends language and customs. Feeling as communication connects cultures once separated into tribes, regions, states, countries, nations, and worlds. In feeling there is no separation. Subsequently, there are no differences. The differences fade in recognition that feelings are the common thread that unify. Through the unified energy field of feeling what's the point of separatism? The only point of separatism is to continue the frequency and vibration of the Duality Programs of fear.

In becoming connected to the consciousness of Oneness you initiate the development and integration of your multiple dimensional levels of your consciousness. Not only through the vibration and frequency of your feeling are you connected to others, you begin to feel within yourself your connection to your many levels of consciousness that live within your physical body. You become the inter-link of conscious communication within and outside of you as you begin to live in a unified field of energy as the Oneness of you.

Becoming a multiple dimensional being in a consciousness of Oneness is recognizing and realizing that all the potentials and the possibilities of your creativity lie within you. You are embarking on a journey of self-discovery that is beyond the limits and the narrowness of your ego's vision of you. There is no time like the present moment to make the choice for yourself. You have experienced the confinement of the duality programming of fear. Feel the feeling. When you feel it, you will know what the "it" is. The "it" is the break-through from the emotional hooks to the programs. Freedom is on the other side in the feeling.

No-Time

No matter how time is perceived from a perspective of past, present, and future, time is really Now. Your body holds all the memories, memorizations, and sounds in your time continuum, right here, right now. Your consciousness and even your unconsciousness draws from your personal time continuum how you will act, react, or behave in this lifetime. Regardless of the perception of linear time, your time is always Now.

You are a compilation of all of your experiences in your time continuum. You are also a collective of your conscious awareness and your unconsciousness in your time continuum. This means that you were a more or a less conscious human in a particular lifetime. As an inter-link within yourself, you interface with your levels of consciousness throughout your time continuum. This interface reflects in your actions and behaviors in your linear periods of time. Most of the interface is done unconsciously, because it is the dynamics of the conditioning. The consciousness of your DNA and your biology is also impacted by the conditioning.

The No-Time is the un-space without the conditioning of time and the programs. This un-space of the No-Time provides an energetic place for you to access the information from your time continuum as an observer, to view and evaluate all the levels of your consciousness. The evaluation process is not infused with judgment. In a manner of speaking, time is suspended so that you may sort through the information, retain what will assist you in the Now and benefit your future Now, and let the rest go. Why take up room with an energy of consciousness that does not serve you?

Therefore, the No-Time is also the energetic place of the "letting go" of the density of any form of consciousness that does not serve your best interests anymore. The No-Time is your un-space of opportunities to choose your changes of consciousness. The No-Time contains no boundaries or limitations. The No-Time contains only flexible parameters as you determine them to be. The un-space of the No-Time is ever expanding as you expand your consciousness. The No-Time is your creation just as you create your life here on this planet. How you use the No-Time and what you create new in your Now is up to you.

Through your feeling, clear of emotions, at the very cellular level in the multiple dimensions of your consciousness. all your memories, memorizations, and sounds are accessed in the un-space of the No-Time. Without a place for fear you empower yourself to produce a more positive, more productive life. You are accessing your Oneness of consciousness. You are at your core.

Your Core

There are no more maps, no more creeds, no more philosophies. From here on in, the directions come straight from the divine. The curriculum is being revealed millisecond by millisecond—invisibly, intuitively, spontaneously, lovingly. As one of Thomas Meto's monks has it,

"Go into your cell and your cell will teach you
everything there is to know." Your cell. Your self.
-Akshara Noor

The Set-Up

The Set-up is the activation of a situation, experience or condition in your life that changes your life at the core. Set-ups are manifested through life altering changes like an illness, a loss or death, or a radical change in your circumstances. As a result of these changes, some dramatic, some subtle, the way you view yourself, others, and the world changes permanently. In the permanency the change can be gradual or sudden. Permanency, in this context, means you can never go back to the old ways of thinking.

As a result of this change in you, you begin to realize that your life does not have a purpose, but is on purpose. Being on purpose is multifaceted and multiple dimensional. The old operating programs do not seem to have the purpose that they did before. In the Set-up time, it can appear that you are totally alone, that you are abandoned, isolated, lost. The fear of being alone may seem overwhelming. Not being understood and not understanding yourself, is part of the dynamics involved in the Set-up. This process encourages you to look within for answers. At the core, beneath the fears, is where the Truth and the clarity reside.

From an outside perspective, the Set-up can look like you and your life have fallen apart. This is part of the clearing process. Metaphorically, it is a spiritual roto-rooter in action. You cannot rise above the emotions without clearing out the Fear Programs at your cellular level.

For example, the abandonment issue is a debilitating fear, which prompts repeated cycles of dysfunction. Whether you play the abandonee or the abandoner, it is still the same fear-based behavior. Whatever your personal script calls for, you can create it at the beginning, middle, or end of your life. Abandonment is a fear issue, like any other fear issue, that can be carried over from lifetime to lifetime in your time continuum. No one wants to repeat this program because it is so very painful and debilitating. Without comprehending that this fear issue or other issues are buried deep in the unconscious, this pattern of behavior is enacted repeatedly.

In the Set-up, using abandonment as the triggering issue for instance, when you go to the core you discover in every time frame your own self-involvement in arranging the abandonment situation. Again, whether abandoner or abandonee, the fear is the same, regardless of the positioning of your role.

The Set-up is the vehicle that allows you to become conscious and to release the old program, no longer to repeat history. In the Set-up you become aware and conscious of your responsibility to your life. You discover that your responsibility is your ability to respond to an issue of fear or not. You have a choice. Without cognition of choice, you simply re-act the issue again and again.

When you reach the core in the Set-up time, you cannot ever again blame anyone else for being responsible for anything that happens in your life. Your responsibility is knowing at the core that your life is in your hands. The outcome of your life comes out in new and more creative directions, not based on old fears and their patterns. So embrace your Set-ups. You wrote them into your scripts to get conscious in the Becoming of Who You Are. Embrace them. Your clarity comes from what you learn about yourself from the Set-ups. Your empowerment comes from releasing the dysfunctional fears.

In the remembering, recalling, and recollecting, the Set-up is to bring to the surface, right from the core, every aspect of your Duality Programs. Every hidden agenda rises to the surface. Every program has two sides to the issue. The abuser, the abusee, the controller, the controlled, the haves and the have-nots, the hater, the hated, everyone has participated in these Duality Programs.

At some point, in some lifetime, you played out each side of the Duality Programs. Through these experiences, you have the opportunity to gain wisdom through your No-Time and your Set-ups. There is No-Time like the present to let go of the repeated lessons, embrace what the lessons have taught you, and move forward. This is how you change your consciousness and the consciousness that lives on the planet. It does not change through repeating the lessons. The lesson is getting it!

From your insight and wisdom gained from your time

continuum, Now is the time to create your life from the expanded frequency and vibration of the Oneness. Now is the time to create new futures. Be your own futurist. Envision and activate a new future that is what you desire, require, and deserve.

Let go of the old "wanty-needy" fear energy. When you say, "I need something," what you say is, "I don't have what it takes." The Truth is, at the core, you and everyone has what it takes. The "it" is your infinite potential and possibilities. When you say, "I want something someday," you are saying to yourself that you are in a lack energy now. From that energy of lack, you are projecting this energy into a future that is based on a foundation of fear that you will never get what you want. The energy of consciousness based on fear only re-creates the pattern of the wanting. Rarely does the wanting become tangible. When it does, the fear from the Take-Away Program manifests the physical take-away. The take-away occurs.

Remember always that your consciousness is energy. Through your energy, you create your life by every thought you think, every word you speak, and every act you act out. Looking at your future of new potentials and possibilities, change your word "want" to "desire." The word "desire" simply means to sire or birth. In your present moment of the Now, what is it that you desire to create for your future? In the Inter-Link and connection to the Universal consciousness of Oneness and your multiple dimensional levels of yourself, your soul, and your spirit, along with your body, know what you require to create for yourself to ascend your consciousness. Living in an energy field of "wanty" keeps you disconnected from your Oneness.

The extension of the "wanty" is the debilitating dysfunctional energy consciousness of "needy." "Needy" is the expanded fear consciousness of the Lack Program. "Needy" is the energy-drainer and victim/victimizer behavior in the consciousness of the Lack Program. "Needy" is a dark, sticky mass of energy that is generated through the Second Chakra. The foundation of this "wanty" reactionary consciousness is housed in the First Chakra. Changing the consciousness from need and "needy" to "requirement" is life-altering. This is a physical planet. Everyone has requirements to live on this planet. By changing to "requirement", your consciousness and the flow of your energy becomes lighter and you become more positively proactive in your life. This may sound simplistic. It is. There is a higher vibrational frequency to "desire" and "require" than there is to the vibrational frequency of "wanty-needy."

The third component to releasing the low-based energy of "wanty-needy" is knowing without doubt and with complete trust of yourself at your core level, that you absolutely without question DESERVE what you DESIRE and REQUIRE to create for yourself in this lifetime. You have no requirement to be "wanty" and "needy", nor do you deserve to live in that field of energy and consciousness.

The old not-deserving fears, so deeply embedded in the Duality Programs, have been perpetuated through a myriad of religious, governmental, and social organizations, from lifetime to lifetime. The fears and the conditioning said, "You do not have enough, will never have enough, and do not deserve enough." This is simply not the Truth. So cancel wanty-needy and acknowledge that you do require, desire, and deserve a productive, creative, and happy life with enough. Whatever enough means to you in your consciousness, and not based on someone's idea of what is enough for you, you are free to manifest more than enough.

At your core you will discover that consciousness of One and Oneness does not mean a singularity. One consciousness is multiple dimensional. It is multi-faceted. You are all aspects of One consciousness. You were separated from the Wholeness of Yourself by the fears and through the manipulation of your consciousness by the separatism paradigm of the duality programming regardless of the lifetime. Your life, your behaviors, and your values were delineated by separatism as a belief system. Not only does it promote the separation of you from others, you became separated from yourself and your core Truth of universal consciousness of Oneness. The vibrational frequency of separatism is intensely dense. Because of this massive density, there is little room or light to expand the consciousness. The thickness of the denseness is fueled by the emotional intensity of the attachment to the fears.

Perfect examples of this denseness are the Nazis, the Skinheads, or any hate groups. The physicality of their consciousness in their First and Second Chakras is thick with fear.

The energy of the separatism paradigm is so fear-based that individuals and groups do not allow themselves to see beyond the fears. The dynamics of the separatism paradigm are judgments of others, not based on the fact of Truth that everyone is connected in the Oneness of consciousness that allows for the multi-faceted expression of humankind.

In the One consciousness there is room for everyone; everyone has value and is valuable. Everyone's essence emanates from the same Source. As long as the separatism paradigm continues, the same old, same old is created over and over. "My way is better than your way." "My God is better than your God." "My life is better than your life." One way is not better or less than another. It just is.

In separating you from others, and others from you, you also become disconnected from yourself, because of the consciousness of the fears. You and your levels of consciousness become splintered into wedges of lives defined as personal, professional, recreational, spiritual, or whatever label you choose to define that particular wedge. Physically and energetically you divide yourself. Energetically and consciously, you use tremendous energy trying to maintain a balance in your life. Maintaining order is almost impossible. That is why you get burned out or sick. You are living through singular aspects of your life, moving in and out of these wedges of consciousness and behaviors that make up your physical reality. This takes a lot of energy to maintain these fields of disconnected consciousness. Singularity is the separatism paradigm. The Oneness of consciousness is the multiple dimensional multi-faceted levels of your consciousness integrated for living your life in Wholeness. You are not separated from others or yourself. One Consciousness transcends and embraces differences without judgment and opposition. In this field of frequency and vibration there is no requirement for hate.

Learning is
A natural acquisition of information
Regardless
If it is being judged as good or bad.

Author

Chapter 4
Self-Consciousness
Questioning, the Shake-Up, Fragmentation

The Spirits of truth and falsehood
Struggle within the heart of man;
Truth born out of the spring of Light,
Falsehood from the well of darkness.
And according as a man inherits truth
So will he avoid darkness.

-from the Manual Discipline
Of the Dead Sea Scrolls

Regardless of your religious ideas, agendas, and belief systems, encountering the information presented here will undoubtedly trigger questions, skepticisms, and criticisms. It is designed to do this. It is designed to move you to question yourself, your assumptions, and your belief systems on all the multiple dimensional levels of your consciousness. You are required, by your choice, to go beyond the third dimensional perspectives of right and wrong, good and bad, and valid and invalid.

Your journey in your Becoming of the Truth of Who You Are is about releasing judgment in any way. It is about questioning everything. It is about questioning what you "think" you believe and do not believe. It is questioning what is comfortable and not comfortable to you. It is questioning what is valuable and not valuable, and it is questioning what serves you and what does not. It is also about your own inner trust and faith as your guide in your quest for answers. The trust and faith part of your quest is most important. The level of difficulty or ease through which your quest takes you through the Becoming absolutely depends upon your faith and trust that the answers are indeed within you. The answers are never outside of you as you have been conditioned to believe. They are within you and nowhere else.

The comprehension of yourself, as being part of the Universal Consciousness of Oneness, unfolds along the journey of self-discovery through the discernment process. Though it may appear that there are challenges and tests, these are your reality benchmarks. As you comprehend that you create these benchmark challenges, you will see these "tests" teach you about yourself. How you work through your lessons and your tests is up to you. You can look at them as challenges or as opportunities to get to your Truth. The choice is up to you. You are the Creator of your life's script and your agreements. As the Creator, you will discover through the process of becoming conscious that you do have choices. When you continue to create through fear, you also discover that your choices are limited or nil. Discernment between your Truth of Universal Consciousness of Oneness and the fear consciousness of duality determines the spectrum of your choices.

The Shake-Up

What begins to happen in your discernment process is that your third dimensional ego and your world as you "think" you know it experiences a shake up. All your ego's old patterns, behaviors, and values begin to be disrupted. Sometimes it may seem that you are falling apart and your that world is crumbling. The ego can only interpret life through fear. Though fear is a narrow band of a dense frequency, the energy emitted from this restricted band is an overpowering field of fear consciousness. This energy of fear feeds the ego. It is the food of consciousness in which the ego is nourished. When threatened, the ego is shaken in its dimension of reality that sees life through the fears. The ego's behavior is based upon the foundation of fear energy. The consciousness of the ego is perfect for third dimension. It cannot live anywhere else.

The ego's consciousness loves to make you righteous and valueless at the same time. The ego is the mastermind of your third dimensional reality. A master of the temporary, and of all opposition, the ego knows that fear is the field of energy in which to manipulate through the programs. When all of the things that the ego thought were valuable no longer appear to have the same value, the ego begins to fight for survival. The ego invents outside conflict to both verify and vilify you at the same time. The ego maintains control from the inside out and the outside in. As your consciousness blends into the One Universal Consciousness, the ego loses its designation as being a separate identity.

The objective of the One Self-Consciousness is the integration of your physical body with your spirit, soul and your divine ego/mind. This is transcension. This is rising above the emotional body that reacts and replays the programs through fears and opposition. Comprehend that the value of your lessons is to see that opposition has no place in the One Consciousness that allows room for everyone.

One Consciousness allows for differences without opposition. In One Consciousness there is no room for conflict and war. You can even agree to disagree. A big difference between One Consciousness and the third dimension of opposition is that it is not necessary for one person or group to hurt, manipulate, or rule another. War simply has no purpose or value.

One Consciousness releases the individual and/or group from dependency on opposition. The reality of duality is absolutely dependent on fear and the reactions of opposition. In One Consciousness, relationships are based on inter-independence of unconditional love, without judgment or conditions. Here, all the energy of the Duality Programs have no place, space, or time to live.

The Duality Programs rely on the opposing forces of right or wrong, male or female, high or low, top or bottom, my way or the highway. Duality, in its nature of opposition, depends upon frames of time in the context of restrictions and boundaries. This energetic field does not allow for holding the energy of the Now or the present moment for an extended period of linear time. Moments of the Now-time are beginning to be experienced through feeling them.

The energy of One Consciousness is living and creating in the

Now. Duality draws its energy from the past, moving it into the current timeframe, with its focus on a future recreated from the past. It is a past/future reality consciousness, regardless of where the consciousness is embedded in your time continuum.

The reality is that the duality field of consciousness is simply recycling the old patterns of control and manipulation in updated versions. Any of the versions, whether in the past, present, or future, are dependent upon the consciousness of separation. Separation or separatism, is the dense band of energetic consciousness that both holds the patterns of opposition in place and also maintains the force of opposition for control and manipulation.

The consciousness of duality itself is dependency through fear. All of the Fear Programs, Judgment, Lack, and Take-Away, are acted out and replayed from lifetime to lifetime; because, the dynamics in this field of energetic consciousness, no matter how the fear is labeled, are dependency and co-dependency, the "wanty-needy" field of energy.

There is no empowerment in dependency, co-dependency, or "wanty-needy." No stand of Truth can be taken by anyone as long as you are dependent or co-dependent. It does not matter if the dependency or co-dependency is in a relationship between two people or two groups. The "wanty-neediness" of dependency and co-dependency require control and manipulation. In this never-ending spiral of duality's consciousness, the ego survives. Survival is not living. It is existing through the timeframes of duality. It is certainly not Lifeing in the energy of the One Consciousness of Self.

Lifeing is using your fullest potential of your energy and consciousness. Lifeing is the embracing of your expanded Universal Consciousness. Lifeing is the potentials and possibilities for creating that which you require, desire, and deserve in the context of creating and manifesting your highest and best from moment to moment. There are no limitations to your creativity, and there are no limitations to how much you can create, or how many times you can change what you create. There are no patterns in which you can get stuck... unless you choose to be stuck. The consciousness of "survival" and "victim" energies has no place in the energetic field of the One Consciousness of Self.

In third dimension, because of the formulas of karma and lessons, your highest and best could be debilitating and dysfunctional. Karma and lessons are integral parts of duality's consciousness. They support punishment and rewards. One Consciousness has no requirements for karma or lessons, unless you choose to create them. In One Consciousness, you are conscious and aware that it is you who are the Creator, the creativity, and the manifestor of your life. You are neither separate, nor separated. You are One within Yourself. You are also part of the All, and you have choice with whom you participate.

Separation and separatism are financed energetically through the Take-Away Program. Whatever investment you make in creating your idea of what you "think" instead of feel is your highest and best, the underlying currency of the fear energy expects it to be taken away at some point in duality's time. Because of your fears of the Take-Away Program, your energy becomes drained and out of focus. Then your energy and your consciousness become disenfranchised. There is a separation within yourself. You cannot be focused and stay in the moment. The energy of worry about losing, or not gaining more, becomes the center of unbalanced attention, instead of maintaining your focus in the moment.

Your life, your energy, your focus, your creativity become fragmented because of the fears, imagined or not. Fragmentation is the dynamics of being separated from within yourself. You are controlled and manipulated through the fear of the Take-Away Program. It is the duality principle of dividing yourself and being conquered by the fears.

Fragmentation

The principle of fragmentation is designed to divide individuals and groups from each other, as well as keeping yourself divided and in opposition to yourself from within. Fragmentation is an implosion of energy, a contraction of consciousness within you that eventually explodes to the surface by the overwhelming fears of the duality programming. As these bands of energy, propelled by the consciousness of fears, are released from within the physical body as streams of energy, it appears you are going in many directions at one time. Energetically, consciously and physically, that is exactly what is happening. The physical body, the emotions, the ego, the spirit, and the soul become out of balance on all their levels of consciousness. Fragmentation is a breakdown and separation of consciousness on all levels. There is no balance of consciousness or connection to each other. There is no awareness of the All of You.

You are fragmented and fragile. In this state of fragility, illness, disease, and emotional disorders are easily created in the physical body. Energy becomes dispersed in multiple directions. The energy is not balanced, and neither is the consciousness. Everything is disjointed, chaotic, and confusing. Turmoil is the manifestation of fragmentation. Anxiety is the turmoil of the fragmentation. Your body is in one place, while your energy and consciousness is separated into many directions. You are fragmented because you are fearful, even when you are not aware of it. Becoming aware is becoming conscious without judgment of yourself or others. What you judge of others is yourself. Fragmentation says you are separate. One Consciousness of Self knows you are not.

Fragmentation is the inability to stay and maintain focus. At times you rely on fragmentation; often you are unaware of it. It becomes your excuse and gives you the ability to live out your excuses. This behavior pattern provides you the excuse to give away your power. Living in fragmentation disenfranchises you because it is disempowering. The disempowering behavior produces the consciousness, servitude, and sacrifice within the programs. Often you sacrifice your life force and energy by giving away your power through excuses, through blame, through belief systems that you accept that do not honor you as One Consciousness of Self.

You are taught this to be controlled and manipulated. You are conditioned to believe the idea that serving your own highest and best is "selfish." The energetic consciousness of "selfish" is used to control you through guilt and unworthiness. The emotional hook of this band of energy is in the First Chakra of the old system. The control and manipulation of this consciousness relies on the fear of not-deserving. The Wordology of "selfish" and "not-deserving" lives in the biology of the First Chakra. The Second or Creative Chakra emits this band of energy which attracts to you from the outside the participants who validate you as "not-deserving" and "selfish." This consciousness of energy is embedded inside of these two Chakras. Fragmentation is being controlled and manipulated by yourself without the awareness of it.

Intervention

Look at your government and welfare systems. These are perfect examples of intervention and manipulation. These interventions and manipulations are cloaked in the idea of what is "best" for someone or a group. These programs fuel the genre of perpetuating servitude and mastery. This serves no one, least of all the ones the system maintains it is helping. How can this be an ideal when it encourages servitude? For example, those who are on welfare are judged as lazy, no-good individuals who continually drain our society, which sets them up for a future of continual failure. This paradigm expects them to exist in this failure consciousness. On the other hand, those who are administering the welfare programs appear to have job security. Their security paradigm is based upon the insecurity consciousness of those on welfare. Both versions of consciousness are illusions. They only appear *real* from the third dimensional perspective of opposition as the manipulated and the manipulators. This paradigm does not support a consciousness of growth, abundance, and prosperity. Those on welfare are fragmented from the other segments of society that appear to have worth and value. This paradigm only perpetuates the Judgment, Lack, and Take-Away Programs.

The misconception is that anyone, group, or institution, can do anything "to" or "for" someone else. The truth is, you cannot do anything "to" or "for" someone else. Whether individually or in groups, everyone equally participates with each other, whether they are consciously aware of their participation or not. Everyone is acting out their role. The idea of doing something "to" or "for" someone is based on manipulation. Whether you are the manipulator or the manipulated, you are equally participating. When you comprehend that you are a participant in every aspect of your life, you take back your power. You listen to yourself at a deeper level of consciousness, aware of your words, actions, and behavioral patterns. You realize that no one is doing anything "to" you or "for" you that you are not allowing. In this field of conscious energy you cannot be "wanty-needy", a "victim", or a "blamer." Life gives you something. It is up to you what you give to your life from the inside out and how you participate.

Participation is an energy exchange of sharing beingness. In the instance of welfare, it is in the guise of sharing. You cannot really share until the consciousness is the same, on the same wavelength, on the same frequency of participation. You do not "share" with welfare. Welfare maintains the person or group in a fragmented status of "less than" and "have-nots", and "no-good", and "not good enough." Many times the question has been asked, "Should the system be reformed?" Consider this: is it time for your consciousness to be re-formed, releasing the idea that people on welfare are a fragmented group of society. There is no unity in fragmentation. There is no field to hold the space for the Oneness of Universal Consciousness.

Self-fragmentation within the individual is that awful emotion of being isolated or alone. You may become completely disenfranchised from your body. Your body is performing your daily functions, but the focus of your consciousness is somewhere else. You "think" you are separated from being supported or connected to any one or any thing. In extreme cases you become so out-of-body, your body breaks down into illness or disease. The worst case scenario is the untimely death by "accident" or illness.

Sometimes the fragmentation is enhanced through the use of drugs. Sometimes being out of body is the draw to stay fragmented, to live outside of your body in a different reality. And sometimes the fragmentation occurs from an illness. The illness may become the focus of the reality. In a sense, the illness or continued use of drugs provides the reason for living in fragmentation. At some point the "turn" occurs whether you turn your life around or it turns into death.

Even in the context that the soul becomes fragmented, there is a method called "soul-retrieving." It is a mechanism devised to integrate the soul back into the body. The Truth of the matter is the soul is not lost. The consciousness of the soul is fragmented within you, and your physical body is out of balance and not in alignment with yourself.

All of those lost parts of self are simply the aspects of your multiple dimensional consciousness that reside in the cellular memories, memorizations and sounds of your body. When you escape into the reality of fragmentation, you are giving away your power. The physical and emotional pain is the body's signal to pay attention to what is happening in your body. When you are balanced, living in the Now, and connected to yourself at your very core level, there is no requirement for the body to produce pain. Therefore, the consciousness of fragmentation has no place, space, or time in your consciousness.

Remember when you said, "I'll be happy when…" or "I used to be great when…but I am not now?" Did you ever consider that you are fragmenting your thoughts about yourself to a future time that has not yet been created and to a past time that may or may not be true? What this does is to fragment you into a field of energy of "used to be" or "waiting for." There is no Lifeing in the past or in the future. Why sacrifice your energy and your creativity to a timeframe that is already done, and to a future timeframe that is not clear? Stay fragmented and you keep yourself separated from the empowerment of clearly creating the life that you deserve to manifest and maintain. Maintaining your life and expanding your consciousness are as important as creating it.

The Duality Programs are layers and layers of consciousness from all your lifetimes. Opposition, take-away, lack, not-deserving, insufficiency, separatism, fragmentation, whatever label you give to any version, they are simply methodologies that have been designed to keep you off balance, out of focus, and disconnected from your own Truth.

Allow yourself the opportunity to feel the essence of Yourself. Get to know yourself from the inside out. Getting to know Who You Are, not what you think you are, or what you have been told you are, or what reflection that you are, means connecting to your Truth. Your Truth is inside of you.

The Term "Lightworker" – Another Form of Separation/Fragmentation

On the planet many have made statements that they are lightworkers. What does this mean? Does being a lightworker mean that yet another group separate from others has been formed? The Truth is your bodies are dense from the layers and layers of the Duality Programs. As you tap into the light (knowledge) about Yourself, at your core cellular levels, in those spaces beneath the quarks, the neutrinos, and the nanos, whatever labels you prefer, these spaces are clear. They are devoid of the programs.

As you journey through these layers of the old programming, and delete them one by one, the density of the old consciousness leaves your body. You become lighter. The lightness, the Light, is the knowledge that you have learned about Yourself. If you want to label yourself a "lightworker", then by all means understand that the work is about "letting go" of the old programs and the old consciousness. It is an individual inside job. Your Light is your knowledge. The density is living in an energy field of ignorance, which is the darkness. Darkness is the practice of ignorance. Light is the absence of ignorance.

Over and over again you have been challenged by the tests that you designed for yourself to learn about you. You designed these tests as your lessons to either continue the programs or complete the lessons in the Now. How do you know you are done? When you no longer are emotionally hooked, which means you are no longer energetically connected to that issue, no matter what anyone outside of you says or does, you are done. For example, when you are no longer available to be a victim, you no longer draw the energy and the persona of the victimizer to you. Lesson complete. End of story. A new chapter unfolds. In the Now ask yourself, "How much more time do you think you require to test myself with the old programs and repeated lessons?" You are the writer, the script, the agreement, the play, and the player in the trauma drama of your Heaven on Earth. You have the choice and you are the maker of your choices. You are your self-consciousness.

Healing is not peeling away
The layers of the onion.
It is unfolding the information
With clarity from within.

Sherry Anshara

Matrix/Template of Limited Consciousness: Grid of the Seven Chakra System

This is a continuing process of recycling old programs, patterns and behaviors–"same old, same old" regardless of time.

Chapter 5
Is True Enough?
The Old Consciousness of the Seven Chakras

Healing occurs
with the shedding of duality
as you align yourself
with the Oneness of the Force.

Sherry Anshara

How and why are you maintained in the old program and patterns? It is very simple. Your consciousness is embedded in a system of seven Chakras. Chakra is the Sanskrit word that means "wheel", which illustrates the flow of energy in a circular motion. For thousands of years, this system has been accepted as your primary centers of energy in your body. All of the Duality Programs of consciousness and the patterns of behavior of the consciousness are embedded in these seven Chakras, as well as encoded in the cells of your entire body.

In Western culture very little is taught about the connection between your Chakras, your consciousness, your behaviors, and your life. How you act, what you do, all your relationships, everything about your life, and everything your life is based upon, past, present and future is enacted from the consciousness that is embedded in your Chakras and your cells, whether you are aware of it or not. All your interactions; and the manifestations of these interactions are generated from the consciousness that lies in these seven Chakras, the systems to which they are connected, and your entire cellular body.

When the consciousness or the flow of energy of your Chakras is not balanced, neither is your body. For example, when your skeletal system is out of alignment, you might go to a chiropractor for an adjustment. The purpose of the adjustment is to align the skeletal system. Proper alignment makes you feel better. You feel better because the proper flow of energy has a beneficial effect on the rest of your body and its physical systems. However, it is only temporary unless you get to the core issue in that spinal column and identify consciously to what Chakra that misalignment is connected and why it is blocked. You cannot change the "how" until you change the "why."

Treatment of the body for illnesses is just that...treatment, not healing. Treatment does not make the connection to the root of the issue causing the illness. Healing comes from making the connection between the illness, the root cause, and making the choice to change the old consciousness.

Until you connect yourself on all levels of your consciousness, physically, emotionally, psychologically, spiritually, and at your ego and soul levels, you continue the cycle of the old, fear-based Duality Programs in this lifetime and the next, and the next, and the next, as before, as before, as before. Duality, as stated previously, supports continuing cycles of function, dysfunction, function, dysfunction, function, dysfunction. The only thing that will stop this cycle is to choose to end the consciousness of duality within yourself. You do not know what that is…yet.

You do not change the duality system, you release it from your consciousness… you release it out of existence.

THE SEVEN CHAKRAS

All of the consciousness in your body is connected to your Chakras through the programs of your biology, DNA, and conditioning. As stated, the Chakras are a wheel or vortex of energy. Energy is consciousness and consciousness is energy. Energy and consciousness also have a frequency and a vibration. When the energy of the vortex of the Chakra has limited motion, it is blocked and so is your consciousness. The vibration for both is dense.

When the energy vortex of the Chakra and the consciousness is flowing, there is expansion in the frequency and vibration. The limitations of the density are released and there is no sense of being "stuck." The frequency and the vibration of the vortex of your Chakra becomes lighter and more expanded, because the energy of your consciousness becomes more expanded.

In your biology is the history of your experiences. Up to the present moment your history is recorded in the cells in every part of your body, including all of your systems and every part of your physical make-up as well as your aura field. These records of consciousness include your memories, memorizations, and the sounds which pertain to them, even though you may have forgotten the experiences. The memories, memorizations, and sounds within the cellular level are specific to not only a locality in the body, but are also connected to specific Chakras.

Your body of consciousness also is connected and inter-linked within itself and its Chakra system to all the frames of time and experiences that you have had, whether you experienced them individually or as part of a group or of the collective consciousness. Awareness is a step in recognizing your connectedness to this inter-link of dimensional consciousness within you.

Without consciousness of the inter-link, there is no consciousness of the inter-connectedness that lives within your body on all your levels of consciousness. When you are not connected and inter-linked within yourself, you cannot be healed on all these levels of consciousness. When you are not connected and inter-linked with yourself on all levels of your consciousness, you cannot be fully and consciously participatory in life. Because of the density of the frequency and vibrational fields of the Duality Programs, it has been a challenge to make the connections to these levels of consciousness.

When a burst of expansion of consciousness occurs, like a near-death experience, out-of-body experience, or a self-revelation, it is difficult because of the duality density to hold the expansion of consciousness for longer than short periods of time. Experiences of the burst or the glimpse are always life-changing.

However, it can contribute to frustration or anger...why should it be so temporary? There is purpose to this burst or glimpse, and even the anger and frustration, because you begin to understand in your knowing that there really is more than what you have been taught. This is an experience of the More. This More experience begins to raise your level of frequency and vibration, even though it may have been for a short moment. In that moment your body feels the difference between the heaviness of the density and the lightness of the expansion of your consciousness.

The DNA programming is both your lineage and your birth-time into a collective consciousness. How you process the consciousness of your life is not just based on the experiences and the cellular memories of your parents and ancestors, but it also includes the memorizations that your parents learned within the collective consciousness in which they participated and into which you were born. '

Every era holds a collective consciousness: the Thirties' economic Depression; the Forties' "World at War;" the Fifties' "if you don't talk about it, it does not exist"; the Sixties' Camelot and the hidden agendas; the Seventies' drugs and the search for meaning; the Eighties' "me" generation and greed; the Nineties' confusion and the prelude to the end with Y2K. All of these decades represented a collected consciousness in which everybody participated, whether they said they did or not. This may appear simplistic. In the One Consciousness it is. In duality consciousness it is complicated. Nonetheless, you are layers of consciousness. As you integrate your consciousness the simplicity becomes evident.

Your parents' consciousness was affected at their cellular level by their memorizations during each decade. Their memorizations eventually became part of your cellular memory in the encoding in your DNA in the decade in which you were born. Your DNA also includes being connected to your family members and their issues in ways that may be expressed as dysfunctions, diseases, disorders and addictions, as well as their predisposition for health, wellness and longevity. Your DNA affects your physical and emotional levels of consciousness. Since DNA is a frequency and vibration, and a field of energy and consciousness, it can be changed.

The programs of conditioning are so obvious that they go unseen and undetected. The conditioning is so taken for granted that it is mistaken for Truth. There is a fine line between true and Truth. True is the accepted consciousness of the time. And "true" is used to manipulate and control. In a specific religion, if you ate meat on Friday, it was a sin. This was true, but not the Truth. It was "true" within the religion only, but it is not Universal Truth.

"Trues" change over time, and the "trues" are dependent upon the illusional control that they have over an individual or a group. The use of "'trues" can be extremely manipulative especially for economic gain. The "trues" are extremely important to the Duality Programs. Embedded in the "trues" are the unseen fears. The unseen fears are the perfect blockers. The fear blockers are the preventative measures to keep you in line in the Duality Programs. With blocks, there is no flow of energy to allow for the flow of your consciousness to expand. "Trues" are not wrong. They are just what they are - true in their context.

Truth is Universal. Truth is Oneness. Within Oneness there is room for everyone. Again, in Truth, there is room to agree and to disagree without going to war, without killing, and without controlling and manipulating someone else's Truth. In Truth there is not even opposition between the idea of positive being good and negative being bad.

In duality, the polarity of energy is oppositional. Because you are polarity, you have negative and positive poles. Without the negative and positive working together, you would not be who you are. So if everything in your life is in the perspective that everything good that happens to you is positive and everything bad that happens to you is negative, you are in a never-ending cycle of peaks and valleys. There is no stability. The poles must be in opposition to each other. However, in Universal Truth, again, there is no opposition.

Consider a shift in consciousness and realize that negative is not bad. It is the inappropriate use of your energy and consciousness that is your valley, and that your appropriate use of your energy and consciousness is your peak. The Truth is, how you use your energy and your consciousness counts. This is the beginning of balancing your polarity into the Oneness of your consciousness. This is a shift.

In this shift the consciousness of your polarity begins to change from the energy of oppositional forces to an alignment of the negative and the positive poles. In this book, this shift of your Becoming is about the multiple dimensional changes of consciousness within you, your biology, your DNA and your conditioning, as well as your polarity of oppositional forces coming into alignment. Without opposition within yourself, you are aligned with the Universal Truth and Oneness. In this frequency and vibration there is no time or space for the Duality Programs.

The First Chakra: Base Foundation

Your First Chakra is located at the base of your spinal column or tailbone. In this Chakra resides the consciousness of all of your fears, ideas, belief systems, agendas, issues about your life, your biological family, and your relationships with yourself and others who are outside of you. All of your interactions and behaviors with yourself, your family, and others are based upon the energy, frequency, and vibration of your consciousness embedded within this Chakra.

When the First Chakra is filled with the consciousness of the fear-based Duality Programs, the participation of your interactions and relationships are fear-based. Every form of fear, whatever you label it, whatever form of Lack, Judgment, or Take-Away, be it separation, inadequacy, and/or not-deserving, is really about you not being loved and you being unlovable. However, you define the lessons along your journey. The Truth is that the only lesson you are required to learn, understand, and comprehend is that you are love, lovable, and deserving of unconditional love.

All of the programs located in this First Chakra of the old system, based on the Duality Programs, are what this one and only lesson is all about - loving yourself unconditionally and letting go

process for clarity and clarification for healing. It is the basics in Healing 101. Diseases and illness related to the manifestations of the fears locked in the First Chakra are colon cancer, hemorrhoids, fissures, lower back pain, pinched nerves, tail-bone misalignments, all lower back issues, even phantom pain. If you don't know which end is up, start at your First Chakra.

The Second Chakra: Generative/Sexual

As you move the focus of your energy and consciousness from the First to the Second Chakra, an incredible dynamic begins to occur. The Second Chakra is your sexual, generative and creative Chakra. From this Chakra comes the genesis of your seed or ideas. Your seed can generate the physical child that you birth, or it can be the idea from the inventor within you that you create, produce, and manifest outside of yourself. Every person, every situation, every event and every condition is created and produced by you. There is nothing in your life that you do not create whether you are conscious or aware of it or not.

Everything in your physical world is the manifestation of your creativity and your creative ideas that are and have been embedded in the consciousness of your Second Chakra. Consider the statement, "That is my worst fear." How many times have you created in your life your worst fear? This is not a judgment or a commentary on you being right or wrong. It is simply a statement about your creativity and the energy of your consciousness that produces it. Is your creativity a manifestation of your fear or of being clear of what you create and manifest?

When your First Chakra is embedded with fears about relationships, you attract through your Second Chakra relationships based on fear. For example, if you are fearful that you will be abandoned, the relationships you create outside of yourself draws that energy. You will draw the perfect person(s) to you that will validate your "need" to be abandoned. Through the course of time, you may notice how many times you have been abandoned.

Rooted in the abandonment issue is the blame game. You have been programmed to believe that it is the persons outside of you that are doing the abandonment to you. That is not the Truth. The be-lame game is a dysfunctional exchange of energy and consciousness. It is very crippling. It is be-ing lame and giving your power away to someone else. The Truth is the others do not really want your power. But the programs of duality force this dysfunctional exchange of energy and consciousness. Because this idea of abandonment is germinated from within your Second Chakra, you then play out the trauma-drama of abandonment, based on the foundation of this abandonment issue housed in the consciousness of your First Chakra.

The fear of abandonment is a major issue in third dimension that gets replayed over and over again, lifetime after lifetime. When it is not cleared from your consciousness before you transition from this Earth plane, you simply carry this consciousness forward to your next lifetime. This is the Universal Truth of any fear. The frequency and vibration of duality in third dimension embrace the energy of fear.

When you make the connection that letting go of any form or label of fear in your First Chakra is directly inter-linked to your creative process, would you not consider that the time has come for you to take back your power and not recreate another version of that Fear Program, whatever it may be?

Since you can create unconsciously all the trauma-drama in your life and lifetimes, consider how incredible your life can be if you choose to release the fears and be an active conscious participant in the creative process of your life. You can choose to draw friends to you through the Law of Attraction and your generative Chakra, people and groups that support and honor you. This is a step in the process of becoming conscious to how you create your life, and healing those old worn-out issues.

Being fully participatory in all of your creativity and creativeness in your life is what it is all about in your ascension of consciousness. You are ascending above the fears. You are no longer allowing yourself to be controlled and manipulated by the disempowerment of the fear-laden Duality Programs that have affected your life, lives, relationships, creativity, and your creative process. It's a beautiful thing.

The ego is the master manipulator of your Second Chakra. The ego takes the information or the consciousness from the First Chakra and uses it to draw or attract (Law of Attraction) relationships, situations, conditions and events into your life. When the information includes the Fear Programs of abuse, abandonment, neglect, and like issues, the ego will create and recreate the same dysfunctional relationships, situations, conditions, and events. Using the consciousness of invalidation to validate your dysfunctional relationships is perfection for the ego because the ego knows the behaviors and the patterns so well.

Knowing the Fear Program so well is the set up for a lifetime and for lifetimes of creating and recreating the same program though different versions, different time frames, different roles, and yet the same. They all may appear differently, even the view may seem different, but the trauma-drama of the issue is still the same. The scenes may change, just like the lifetimes, but the play is still the trauma-drama. Your ego only knows what to create from the history in the cellular memory, memorizations, and sounds associated with the events and the issues that reside in the First Chakra. Most of your ego's creativity and creations are brought to life by you unconsciously. This is your unconscious consciousness.

The energy of the victim/victimizer, abuser/abusee, manipulator/manipulated, master/slave programs is enacted from your Second Chakra. Through the Law Of Attraction, if one or all of duality's fear-based programs are part of your cellular memory or memorization of consciousness that has not been cleared, you can be guaranteed that in whatever Duality Program you are holding onto, you will play out your part. You have no other choice until you choose to go "into" the consciousness as the observer of your part, to see who has played with you and know they were as much locked into the Fear Programs as you had been.

Now as the observer, you can choose to release your emotional hooks to the issues and let them go. This is the time for the forgiveness of the issues. Forgiveness simply means *for you to give yourself this opportunity* to be the observer, witness the events, see all the players, and give yourself permission to let go of the energy and the consciousness connected to it. You can then release the issue from your cellular memory, memorization, and sound, and move forward in your life, free and clear. You can do this. Your commitment to healing and being free from the issues and fears begins in these first two Chakras of the old system.

All of the diseases, dysfunctions, malfunctions, and pain in the lower parts of your body result from this unconscious consciousness buried in the cells within the locality of these Chakras. When your life force is not being supported, your creativity is not being nurtured, and you are not honoring your life because of the fears, your life force becomes ill or diseased. Illness or diseases, such as ovarian cancer, prostate cancer, cysts, kidney and bladder infections, intestinal tract problems., can be created wherever your physical and emotional system is the weakest. These physical problems are actualized in the body as a result of not being conscious in your First and Second Chakras.

The intriguing aspects about the Second Chakra are the correlation between your left side, your female consciousness, and your right side, your male consciousness. In actuality, the physical body at this point in time on the planet is male. This has nothing to do with gender, sexuality, or sexual preference. It simply has to do with consciousness. The male is the manifestor, bringing your idea or seed into the physical realm of third dimension. The body is the physical manifestation of the male consciousness.

The female energy is your consciousness of your spirit. This is the energy force that gives birth to your idea or seed. When your spirit is shut down by the consciousness of fear, the male creativity can only create based on the fears. There is no alignment in this consciousness of fear for the male physical body and the female spirit of consciousness to work together in harmony and peace. Opposition and war is the rule and force of the consciousness.

This time of transformation or transcension is about the female spiritual consciousness uniting in the physical form with the male body. This is, in a metaphoric sense, the sacrament of marriage of consciousness, uniting the male and female together in one body of consciousness. Without this union, healing the child-within from all of the fears can never be completely achieved. Healing only parts of the wounds of the child is simply using temporary Band-Aids.

The sacredness of healing the male, the female, and the child-within as an integrated being in the Oneness in your own consciousness is what is propelling the ascension of your consciousness. Uniting your consciousness with your soul completes the integration of your male, female, and child-within joining a fourth dimension into the physical body. Grounding the life force of your soul through your physical body, and the union of these consciousnesses releases you from the density of the old consciousness of third dimension. More new dimensions, new realities, new creativities - not based on the old fear-based Duality Programs - are now your possibilities and potentials. Your choices are unlimited.

The Third Chakra: Solar Plexus/Child Within

As you continue to empower yourself by healing the emotional issues in the First and Second Chakras, your energy force is ascending, and you become more conscious about yourself, your creative process, and your participation in life. As you integrate through this sacred marriage of the energy and consciousness of your male and female in your physical body, you re-birth the child-within you.

This child represents all of the children from all of your lifetimes of experiences and relationships, events, and situations in which you participated. Your child, as the representative of these children, holds the memories, memorizations, and sounds of the joys and the traumas of all these times. This child is your resource for healing the fears and emotions held within your physical body. It is time to bring your child into the Light and be conscious together.

Your child, through this union, holds the energy force and consciousness of the childlike self-discoverer of life. This child remembers, without fear, the joy and the fun of your creative process. This child remembers the pursuit of discovery without fear. This child remembers how to imagine, how to dream, how to vision, and how to connect with your spirit and your soul without question. Your inner-child of this union is your Light. This child-within you is your child of the Godness within you. This child is your Christed Consciousness. Through the eyes of this child you see the many levels of your participation, not just the limited versions of the third dimensional views.

Your solar plexus is the place underneath your heart where your child-within you lives. When that child's life is lived through the fears embedded in your First Chakra, the creation from the Second Chakra is more painful for your child than you can imagine. The emotional pain that you experience is also being experienced by the child-within you. The emotions of the painful history of the experience can repeatedly be remembered and relived over and over again by you through your child-within. What your child remembers, you remember, and you relive it together, even though you are the adult.

Childish behavior is a reaction to the pain of your inner-child. The reaction is the cover-up and the illusional protection from your ego in the adult body. The ego and the adult both "need" to survive. They only survive because of the child-within. It is the survival consciousness of the child-within that provides the life force to the adult and the ego to continue the journey in the search for healing and clarity. The adult and ego "think" they are in control. What they are controlling is the illusion. The Truth is realized when the child is respected, recognized, and received as a fully functioning member within your adult male and female in conscious unity. There is empowerment to continue the journey without pain, fear, and/or limitations. Survival is a part of the consciousness of the Lack Program.

With the emotional scars and fears cleared from the First Chakra, and as this clear energy rises into the Second Chakra, the creative force is open and expanded to create into your physical world new ideas for a more productive life. With the child-within as an integral part of your creative force, there are no requirements to hold onto the illusional fears that block your creativity. The child and the adult are free to explore all possibilities and potentials. There is no room for the consciousness of lack and survival in this Union of Consciousness.

There is no time, space, or place for the fear-based ego to live.

Your childlike energy is the inter-link for your female and male to integrate and birth your Christed Consciousness into your physical body. Jesus represents the child of God. Your child-within is the child of God within you birthed through the conscious healing and integration of your female spirit and male body. This brings into unity the Father, the spirit and the child as One, Lifeing together in your one physical body with your soul/divine mind. Through this union, your energy begins to synchronize with Universal Consciousness and rises up to meet your heart.

The Fourth: Chakra-Heart

Our Father who art in Heaven, hallowed be Thy Name. The body physical is male and is the producer into the physical of creativity. When you look at the word "heart" you will see that it spells, "he-ART." Through your heart that is healed in the integration of your male (physical) body, your female (spirit), and your inner-child, you create more on the canvas of your life. You are the conceptualizer, the artist, and the canvas. You can choose how you paint your life, including those who participate with you or not.

On this canvas of your life is the "hallowed be Your Name." Directing your creative energy from your generative Chakra, based on your foundation without fear, embracing your integration of your male-female with your inner-child, you create from the heart that is the Godness within you.

Lifeing and creating through your heart is healing in itself. There is no inner conflict or turmoil no matter what is happening outside of you.

Matters of the Heart
Love is all that Matters
We are the Matter
Of all living
Matter that you live
Your living Matters
To all. We all are One

Wei Chen

As Wei Chen expressed in this beautiful poem, all that really matters is what matters to you from your healed heart. And through your heart you continue the ascension of your consciousness as well, as you begin to shift out of the old paradigm of the third dimensional seven Chakras that are embedded with the fears of the Duality Programs.

All of the diseases, afflictions, or dysfunctions in the location of the Heart Chakra - whether heart attacks, respiratory issues, lung problems, circulatory problems, etc. - result from the broken heart of the inner-child. The ego does not allow the child to know that there are other alternatives. The ego-child thinks he or she has no other alternative. In your script or agreement that you write for yourself through your journey on Earth, you always include an escape clause.

When you look at the rate of heart disease and death by the malfunctions of the heart, it is the child-within the adult body that uses the escape clause to check out. When you do this, remember that what you do not heal through your heart before you leave this Earth plane, the fine print in the clause states, "...subject to the reincarnation program." Trust that you will remember yourself at some point and say, "Enough is enough. I choose to heal through my heart."

The four chambers of the heart metaphorically represent the four dimensions of your consciousness of your male (physical body), your female (spirit), your child-within, and your soul. When you use your heart as the energizing force, from a cleared foundation of creativity with the openness of the child-within you, your creativity is expressed through unconditional love. There is no requirement to allow old emotions and old fears to interfere with your creativity. All directions from your heart are open and clear to participate in the expression of your artistry.

The rise of your energy and consciousness from your healed heart into your Fifth Chakra, your throat, provides the vocal pathway for you to begin to speak your Truth.

The Fifth Chakra: Throat

The Truth shall set you free. Speaking your Truth absolutely sets you free. When you are speaking from your heart, your words are without judgment. When you judge others, you are really speaking words that are judging you. This is the Truth. When you begin to speak your Truth without judgment and with kindness and compassion, your energy begins to flow with continuity. There are no words of fear coming out of your mouth. When you speak with judgment, fear traps the flow of your energy, and it does not move freely through your body or your Chakras.

Your feet, when you speak through the energy of fear, get stuck. You know that emotion: "I can't move forward"; "I'm stuck"; "I'm going in circles." What is happening is that you really are stuck. You have been choked by fear. The energy in your feet is also choked and you are not moving forward. Your feet are interlinked and connected to your Throat Chakra.

Physical problems in your feet such as broken bones, bunions, in-grown toenails, blisters, bone spurs, weak ankles, etc., are all emotional issues housed in the Throat Chakra that stop the flow of energy for you to move forward in your life. Linear time moves on but your life becomes stagnant, stuck somewhere in a fear of the Judgment, Lack, or Take-Away Programs. Energetically your feet are frozen in the timeframe of the fear issue.

The words that you speak from your Throat Chakra, consciously or unconsciously, when based in fear, become statements of self-prophesy: "I don't deserve"; "I am not good enough"; "No one will ever love me"; "I don't have the right looks"; etc. Whatever the declarations the Throat Chakra speaks, whether spoken silently or out loud, the body hears. The fears of the First Chakra are produced through the generative Chakra, the child-within hides, the heart is hurting, the learned self-hating words from the Throat Chakra get stuck in the feet, and your body unconsciously relives and reenacts the old programs. The Chakras and the consciousness within the Chakras are closed. You are not moving forward in your life.

Learning to speak your Truth with kindness and compassion from your heart opens up your Chakra fields of energies. As this occurs, you begin to move forward into a future from the present moment, speaking your words with clarity and clarification. Others begin to notice that something extraordinary has begun to happen. You are "taking your stand" and "speaking your Truth" without emitting an energy of opposition.

You are empowering yourself by accepting that Who You Are and what you say has meaning and purpose. You have meaning and you have purpose. As you clear the consciousness within your Chakras, your body physical heals. Your body knows what to do. When you get out of your own way, then you can thank your ego for being a great teacher. You will recognize the time has arrived to go beyond the fears and take command of yourself. Speaking your Truth into the physical is the energy that empowers you.

You speak without fear from a clear foundation. You speak your creativity with your healed inner-child through your heart. You are aligning as One within yourself. What you speak you make so. Whether you abuse yourself or support yourself, your words tell you where you are, where you have been, and where you are going. The words are the sounds, the vibrations, the frequencies of you, expressed.

The old paradigm looks at the Throat Chakra as a tool of the body to speak, to sing, to yell, to cry, to emit sound, particularly words. The deeper purpose for the Throat Chakra is that it provides a vocal avenue for cellular sound releases for all parts of your body to express. For instance, at a particular time in your life, you may have been frightened, shocked, traumatized, or felt joy and happiness. The sounds and their associated timeframes of these experiences, whether trauma or joy, are memorized by you in the different areas of your body associated with the experiences.

In the healing process, when a sound is equated to a trauma, that sound is stored as a cellular memorization. During the healing process, that particular sound, emitted from the Throat Chakra, provides a physical expression for the sound to be released from the part of the body that was traumatized. For example, when a person is in an accident and hurts a leg, the leg memorizes the accident, the sound equated to the accident, and the pain. Both are embedded in the cellular level of the leg. When only a physical healing occurs, there is still pain in the leg. The pain is the emotion and sound of the accident stuck in cellular memorization of the leg from the timeframe of the accident. Releasing the sound and the frequency of the pain through cellular release, provides the person with the opportunity to let go of the trauma, the timeframe, the sound, and the pain. Your Throat Chakra is the avenue for the release of the sound of the pain.

Through sound and frequency, the Throat Chakra is a key link to the consciousness embedded in the other Chakras. It gives sound to healing. Healing is a sound. Healing is a frequency. Everything in your body, the cells, the systems, the consciousness, are all versions of sound, and have their own frequency. When your frequency and sound are out of balance, it is impossible to align your body of consciousness in the physical. Your body physical is what houses all your vibrations, all your frequencies, all your tones. Every type of sound that you are is stored in your body, whether you are conscious of it or not.

The importance of your Throat Chakra is expressed through the words you communicate to yourself and to others. When your words are spoken in a frequency of fear, like self-sabotage, self-loathing, and less-than, your body reacts to this frequency. Your energy becomes focused in a sound of depression and/or illness, or a state of dis-ease, which may lead to a more serious illness. The vibration and frequency of your words impact your life. In the duality paradigm, polarity is described as either positive or negative. The conscious energy of your vibration and frequency has nothing to do with being positive or negative. However, it does have to do with the focus of your conscious energy being either appropriate through your Higher Consciousness or inappropriate through the Duality Programs. When you use inappropriate words that hold a lower-based frequency of vibration, your actions and behaviors are based on fear. The creative process of your actions and behaviors are predicated upon the frequency and vibration of your words and sounds. Whether you act appropriately or inappropriately is indicative of your frequency and vibration of consciousness. What comes out of your Throat Chakra is your consciousness.

Healing your Throat Chakra allows you to begin to heal your entire body through the physical vibrations of sound. Whether silent or spoken to your female spirit, male physical body, child-within and your soul, you release the frequencies of emotions and fears, sounding out the integrated frequencies and vibrations from illness to healing.

Speaking your Truth is vital to your life. Speaking your Truth through kindness and compassion, and not through the fear-based Duality Program of judgment, creates an energy of vitality. Your consciousness expands. You begin the vibrational ascension of consciousness in the most practical terms to your life.

Speaking your Truth through unconditional love, you initiate the frequency that you indeed are the Creator and manifestor of your life and your journey. You become in the Becoming the active participator/Creator, no longer the re-actor enmeshed in the process of the old consciousness. From your healed Throat Chakra your body vibrates; your body listens; your cells respond to the sound of the God within you, spoken by you, either verbally or non-verbally. You are speaking your Truth. You are the sound of your own music.

Your Truth, spoken by you from your Throat Chakra, raises your frequency and vibration of consciousness. You begin to hear and see more clearly. Your vibration and frequency is ascending.

The Sixth Chakra: Third Eye

From your Third Eye come visions from your Higher Self. When your Third Eye is closed, your intuitive energy field is shut down. Your field of energy is directed completely by your ego. Your life is lived ingrained in the Duality Programs from your First Chakra, and your creative process is produced outside of you from the fear foundation emanating from your First Chakra. The base of your creative energy is activated through your ego's version of right and wrong. Remember that your ego sets you up in this continuing pattern of making you "right" and making you "wrong." This pattern continues through lifetimes, until your Higher Self makes the connection through your Third Eye.

Usually the Third Eye is activated through some circumstance such as an illness, accident or life-altering experience. It can also be opened through intention. As the Third Eye is opened, your view of the world changes. You begin to see beyond the limitations of your third dimensional world. You may begin to see auras, angels, visions, or you may experience realms around you that cannot be defined in third dimensional terms.

Children, particularly the Indigo children (children of a higher vibrational consciousness), under the age of four have their Third Eye open. It is not uncommon for them to talk about imaginary friends, seeing lights around people, or having visitations from deceased loved ones that they never really knew in their lifetime. You may have a remembering in your body of these types of experiences from childhood.

Children's Third Eyes become closed down through the conditioning of the Fear Programs. Their creative process from their Higher Consciousness is shut down as they grow up. Their bodies grow up chronologically, but their Higher Consciousness is not allowed to grow within the adult body. Allowing yourself to let go of the fears from the programming will allow your Third Eye to open up again.

When the Third Eye is not connected to the rest of the body and the other Chakras, the vision for your life is very limited. It is lived within boundaries and limitations that keep you in the low-based energies of the Judgment, Lack, and Take-Away Programs. As you are willing to open your Third Eye and connect it to the rest of your body and your Chakras, the practicality of miracles begin to occur in your life.

As you direct and focus your energy from your Third Eye into your First Chakra, you will begin to see the illusion of the fears and how they have controlled and manipulated your life. As you do this, you are breaking through the painful experiences locked within the fears of the foundation of your First Chakra. The more light, which is your knowledge that is focused into your First Chakra, the more you begin to take back your life force. Your foundation changes. Fear can no longer control your life. You begin to rise above the fear and the emotions attached to it.

As the light of the Third Eye clears out the old fears in your First Chakra, something quite extraordinary begins to happen in your Second Chakra. New creative juices, like the elixirs of life, begin to flow. You begin to comprehend that you are in charge of all your creative processes. You begin to see through your Third Eye that it is you, and only you, that creates everything from within you. You see that everything and everyone outside of you is created by you to learn about yourself. Yes, that means everything and everyone, even the ones you do not like. All the experiences in your life you absolutely created. Good, bad, or indifferent has nothing to do with it.

As you see this through the expanded sight of your Third Eye, the emotional hooks that you once had to someone, to some thing, to some situation, now represent the lesson. At this point, the emotional hooks are released and you begin to take back your power because of your expanded vision of yourself.

Your creative process changes. You know for sure, and without doubt, that it is You who are the creative source of your life. You will recognize that it is You who makes the difference in your life and no one else. You comprehend that no one can do anything to you or for you. You are a participant, but now you are conscious of it, and you see it. This is the empowerment of your creative process. Your creative process is no longer based upon fear.

You have come to the realization that what you create in your future is now no longer a future based on your past programs, behaviors, and actions. The predictable past/future starts to dissolve. At this point you may feel you are going into a void. You are. This void is the place and space of the No-Time. This No-Time or Void is your place of opportunity to expand the vision of yourself with the sight of your Third Eye.

Remember those dreams that you had as a child or as an adult that you held within you? In this No-Time and Void you are giving yourself (no one gives it to you), the opportunity to re-write your script and produce a new future directed from the vision of your Third Eye through your generative/creative Second Chakra.

You are the creator, the creativity, the creation, the implementer, and the manifestor of your life. In truth, your life is not based on someone else's idea, program, or version of how you are supposed to be. How you create your life is up to you. Empowerment can be no other way. You allow yourself to be creative through the intended energy of your desires (to birth), to bring into the physical reality that which you have known all along is inside of you, that you deserve (of service) to create for yourself. You create a life that is your highest and best.

As the vision of your Third Eye flows through your Third Chakra, which represents the inner-child, distinguishable from the childish ego, rebirths. The view of your world around you, the world itself outside of you, and your relationship to all of it transforms. Your inner-child is awakened with the insight of your Third Eye. Your insight is your real sight. The inner-child, hidden under the weight of the fears, the illusions, and the trauma-dramas emerges. The adult and the child "see" as One.

This step in your awakening allows you to become vulnerable. Vulnerability is not weakness. It is your strength. All of the walls that you have built around you from lifetime to lifetime appeared to have kept you safe. However, these walls have held you captive inside an illusional place of safety and security. It walled up your feelings, which are your Truth. Your emotions held you in bondage from knowing, understanding, or comprehending Who You Really Are.

This illusional bondage was based on the fears of the old programs embedded in your First Chakra. You created the walls from the fears through your Second Chakra, and your child was held captive. The walls that pretended safety kept the vision of your life narrow and full of fear. Whatever the fears that swirled around the hidden inner-child, these fears cut deep into your child's soul, as your spirit and your physical body became disconnected and fragmented.

This fragmentation of your soul and spirit from your physical body and your inner-child was supported through the conditioning and the Duality Programs of control and manipulation. The outside world said, "You needed an emissary or go-between, between you and God." Someone outside of you would have to save you because you had no power, and you are not worthy to have your own power. As long as you stayed within these walls and in the consciousness of your not-knowing, you could be controlled and manipulated, lifetime to lifetime. Call it karma, call it reincarnation, call it lessons. You can name it anything, but the fact is, you are still inside the wall.

Your Light is your knowledge. Embrace the energy of your Third Eye's light into your Third Chakra. Your inner-child sees and feels that vulnerability is strength and courage. Your inner-child can come out to play with expanded views and enlightened visions for your adult life.

As the walls come down, you see the divineness of your life, your creativity, and your participation. As you do this, all the blocking energies of the crippling blame-games, guilties, less than's, why me's, poor me's, any and all versions of victim, begin to disintegrate. Your Light and your knowledge are your divine equalizer.

Your child rises to your surface consciousness and begins to integrate into your adult body, giving your adult a new lease on life. Your adult/child sees things differently. Your adult/child sees that the fears blocked all your energies in your creative process. With your child released, you initiate the journey of self-discovery that is in alignment through the energy of your spirit and the passion from your soul.

It does not matter at what age you do this, as long as you make the commitment to release your inner-child. This is healing with your child at your core. You are integrating. This integration and healing is multiple dimensional in your time continuum. This child-within, as I have said, represents all of the children, from all of your lives, through all of your experiences. Integration is empowerment.

As your child awakens with new vision from your Third Eye,

your enlightened energy ascends into your Heart Chakra filling it with your light and knowledge and a heart-awakening occurs. Sometimes this heart-awakening is subtle, and sometimes, it is quite dramatic. It does not matter. What matters is the energy that is emitted from the Heart Chakra.

The Heart of the Matter
Is the Matter
Of the Heart
The only place
To start
Is what Matters
To the Heart.
Wei Chen

You give yourself permission to love yourself unconditionally, without exception with the joining of the enlightened energy of vision of your child and your heart. All the matters of your life and lifetimes no longer matter. What matters is that you are giving yourself permission to heal the pain, the perceptions, and the programs that engulfed you in the turmoils and trauma-dramas of the third dimension.

The four chambers of the heart are symbolic of the four directions and so above, so below. Look at all the directions that the energy of your heart has flowed or been blocked. The blocked energy has manifested in heart conditions, heart attacks, broken hearts, all the afflictions designated as heart wrenching. Not being loved is the Truth of all conditions at the core of a broken heart.

When you are not loved, all of this broken energy becomes dispersed as it seeks to be loved. However, what occurs is that this broken heart settles for an energy that is based on a love-energy that reflects your ego's conditions. The conditions are founded on the perceptions of love that are controlling and manipulating. If you do this, you will get "this much love", based on what "this much love" means outside of you

The abuser/abusee, the victim/victimizer and the controller/controlled all "live" off this fear-based idea of love. Whatever direction you may be going, it is directed through this fear-based concept of love. It does not work, although it may appear to be working. If, in Truth it was working, then why do so many people feel lonely and unfulfilled? Underneath, the heart is broken.

With the vision of a healed inner-child, focusing your light from your Third Eye directs the energy from your heart from a new foundation, with new creativity, from the present moment into a clear and healed future. As you allow your healed heart energy to expand the direction of your focus, the focus of your life expands. You begin to put your heart into your life with passion. You fall in love with yourself.

When you do this, you give others the opportunity to love you or not. And if they do not, oh well. It has nothing to do with you. What matters is that you love yourself because you have stopped judging yourself by other people's standards of you. When you do this, you realize that you have stopped judging others.

As your life becomes heart-centered, balance becomes the center of your life. You will not be caught up in the trauma-drama. Trauma-dramas are draining, ego-based energy. The trauma-drama is like having sharp hooks dug into your heart. Seeing through the vision of your Third Eye guides your heart on your path toward inner-peace. The alignment of your heart with the First, Second, Third, and Sixth Chakra creates peace and harmony from the inside out. You are now at the heart of the matter of your energy.

From the heart of the matter to your Throat Chakra, the Fifth Chakra, is the part of your journey where you learn to speak your Truth with your Third Eye illuminating your Light and soul, which is your Knowledge inside of you. All the words you speak, or have spoken, are all about you. You start to see the words you use. What words you use tell so much about you, your history, your story, your fears, and your Truth.

Some words are self-fulfilling prophetic words. At times, the words you used sabotaged you, and sometimes, they enlightened you. The sabotage words imprisoned you behind the walls of the not-deserving, not good enough Lack Program. Maybe even the words you used defined the idea that you were being held in a karmic debt/repayment cycle that would never allow you to break through and release yourself. Remember that words are energy. Like Captain Picard said on Star Trek, what you say, you "make it so."

Receiving the energy of your Third Eye into your Throat Chakra releases the words of fear. You begin to see the words of kindness and compassion that you speak, first for yourself and then for others. Your vocabulary changes and "Wordology is your Biology" becomes you.

You can see which words that no longer serve you. Since your words come through your heart with the energy of your enlightened inner-child, with a light force generated with new creativity, you move forward in life. There is no block to keep you stuck. Your feet move you forward with ease and you are standing on happy feet. Your ankles are no longer burdened with the consciousness of not being supported from the outside. You realize that your support comes from within you.

Being brought to your knees by outside influences that do not serve your highest and best good no longer serves you and your knees become more flexible. The upper part of your legs, down to your feet, connected to the trunk of your body, becomes grounded through your enlightened Knowledge about yourself. An integration with your higher vision is taking place in your physical body and throughout your Chakra System. Your life is Becoming with full participation. You see it. You say it. You create it. You Become.

The Seventh: Chakra-Crown

With your Third Eye open, you now allow yourself to make the visual connection to your Higher Self at your crown, or Seventh Chakra. Everyone has a soft spot on the top of their head, but until now we were not aware what its purpose was. It has a two-fold purpose. As you open the soft-spot, you allow all of the fear-based energy to flow up and out of your body to be released. As this occurs, the energy of the soft-spot awakens and expands. As this happens, your Higher Self connects to your physical body. Now you can allow yourself to see the face of your Higher Self. It is You.

The miracle and the practicality of this is that it allows your Higher Self to connect and integrate through your Third Eye into your Throat Chakra. Then it connects and integrates through your Heart Chakra, your child-within Third Chakra, your Second Chakra and your First Chakra, through your arms and legs, right down to your feet, grounding your Higher Self into your physical body. This is transformation and ascension at the same time. It is transcension. Duality begins to disappear, and this is the set up ...for what is next.

Before we get to what is next, you must comprehend that at some point in your life, and usually more times than not, to escape the trauma-dramas of the fears, you go out of body and live somewhere else. When this happens, the body physical is at risk. Many people say that when they go out of body, they are really connecting to their Higher Self. The Truth is, they are not only avoiding their physical self, they are avoiding their Higher Self. The out-of-body experiences and the near-death experiences are all escape clauses in your scripts or contracts.

The Truth of Lifeing with your Higher Self is grounding your Seventh Chakra into your body physical with the integration and alignment of your male body, your female spirit, and your inner-child with your soul. In this alignment of the consciousness within the Seven Chakras and throughout the cells comprising your body, including the DNA, you have the potential to open the physicality of the Thirteen Chakras on this planet of duality. It is time To become the activator of your own personal paradigm shift. The shift happens one person at a time. From a singularity of one in duality, you transcend to the multiple dimensional one of You.

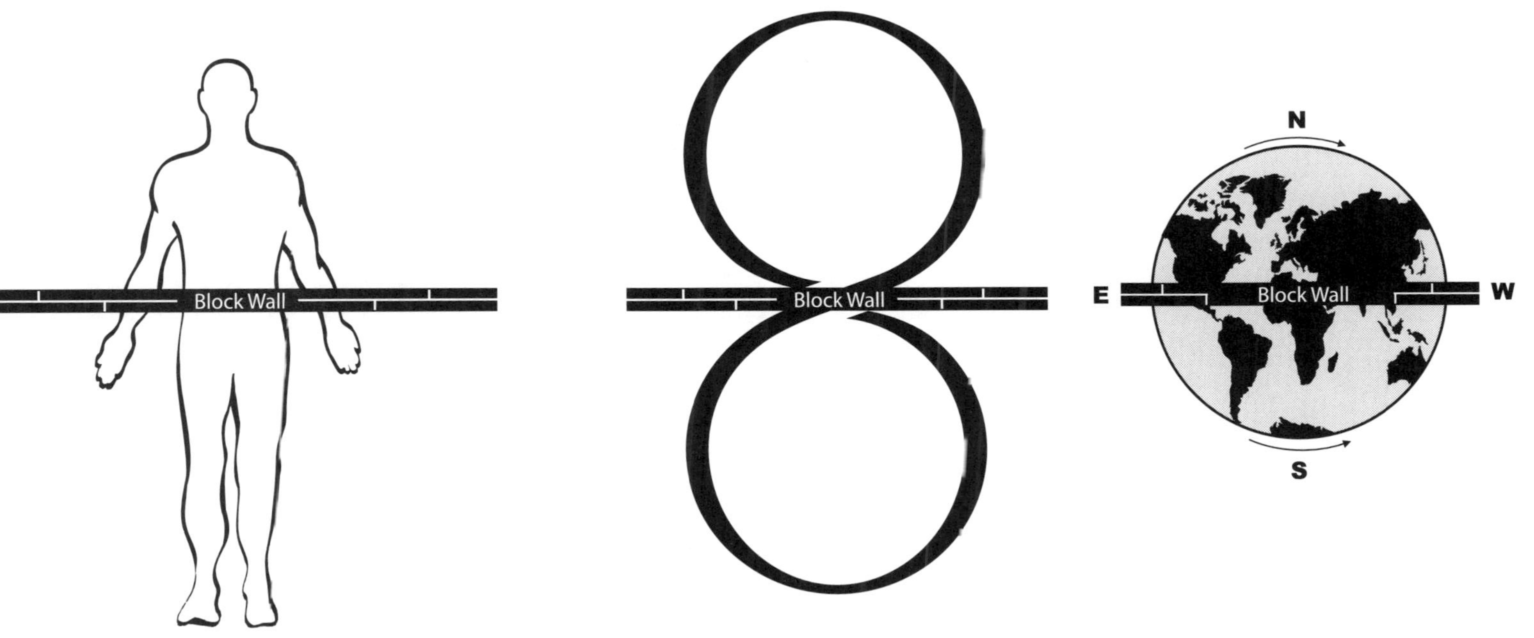

The Limited Body of Consciousness in the 3rd Dimension
The Block Wall

Man in the world of history is like a seed in the ground, an embryo in the womb. His full potential is not at all evident here. No phenomenological analysis of the grain of corn can reveal the nature of the maize plant. So also no amount of biology, psychology, sociology, and history, can reveal to us the true nature of man.

Paulos Mar Gregorios
Cosmic Man, The Divine Presence

Chapter 6

A Paradigm Shift, the Breakthrough

Moving Through the Consciousness of the Block Wall

The spirits of truth and falsehood
Struggle within the heart of man;
Truth born out of the spring of Light,
Falsehood from the well of darkness.
And according as a man inherits truth
So will he avoid darkness.

-from the Manual of Discipline of the Dead Sea Scrolls

Man is an electromagnetic animal
And is subject to those forces
That affect all forms of life existing on Earth.
Man's electromagnetic system is contained
Within his biophysical makeup
And affects the total behavior of not only the body...
Also changes in mental activities
And the electrical biochemical operation of his system.

Albert Roy Davis/Walter C. Rawls, Jr.
Magnetism and Its Effects on the Living System

The Eighth Chakra, the Chakra that is above the crown of your head, is the segue to activating the thirteen Chakras. The Eighth Chakra in your old paradigm of third dimension metaphorically represents the sideways figure "8." It embodies the consciousness of infinity.

The figure eight, the sign of infinity from the viewpoint of duality, depicts the movement of your energy in a cycle of good and bad, high and low, right and wrong, death and rebirth, lessons and reincarnation. In a manner of speaking, both sides of the field of energy are pinched in the middle. Whatever side of the electro-magnetic field that you are living in would appear to the outside that you are being either negative or positive. Though it may appear you are on one side or the other, you really are not.

In the Duality Programs, the polarity of the energy and the consciousness is in opposition. However, regardless of the dichotomy of this polarity, the programs are still the same. For instance, if you are caught up in a program of abuse, at some points in your linear lifetimes you will play out both sides, the abuser and the abusee. This is how the cycle of infinity works in third dimension. You will work and live through both poles of consciousness through the programs, the lessons and the reincarnations. In duality there can be no other way.

When you turn the infinity symbol, aligning it from top to bottom, you will see how it aligns with the electro-magnetic field of the Earth and your Earth-body. The Northern aspect of polarity moves in a clock-wise rotation. The Southern Hemisphere moves in counter-clockwise rotation. In the middle, the two fields come together. This field is dense and taut, and is known as the Block Wall. Through third dimension and its linear time, your consciousness has always encountered both the metaphoric and the actual physicality of this Block Wall.

This Block Wall holds the energy of the cyclic pattern of fear. Phrases like, "I am up against the wall.", "I can't break through the wall.", "I put up a wall to protect myself.", "Why are they blocking me out?" have sentenced you to a consciousness of duality based on the fears of the Judgment, Lack, and Take-Away Programs. As long as the consciousness of this cycle of infinity holds you in this pattern of duality, you will always hit the Wall at one point or another. The Wall is a consciousness.

At your body's mid-point is your navel which is equivalent to the Earth's equator. This magnetic mid-point is the Block Wall where the opposing magnetic energy fields come together. Comparatively, on the human body an electrical equator is where the electrical voltage shifts from positive to negative. At these Walls, there is a 180 degree phase change. In a sense, it is a two-way highway with counter-clockwise and clockwise spin of electromagnetic energies. The electromagnetic energies hold the consciousness of duality and opposition.

At the end of the Wall, a vortex geometrically and perfectly spirals out each side or end. As the duality of the clockwise and counter-clockwise fields is altered, they will no longer be going in opposite directions. They will be moving in the same upward direction. As the spirals of energy and consciousness move in an upward direction together, the Block Wall is dissolved. The spiral of energy that previously had moved in opposite directions will merge as One field of energy and consciousness.

The new alignment of the energy fields, flowing clockwise and counter-clockwise in the same direction at the same rate, rises from the soles of the feet up through your entire body. A transfiguration of your spiritual-electromagnetic frequency within your physical body occurs. You are empowered with an electro-magnetic field of energy that no longer requires you to maintain a polarity of oppositional consciousness with the energy of your spirit, your soul, your inner-child and the alignment of your male and female within you. All are integrated into One Consciousness, This alignment activates your new Thirteen Chakra System, and your body transmutes the old Block Wall. These changes will affect the dynamics of consciousness on this planet.

Visualize a picture of the Earth, analogous to the human body, drawn on a sheet of paper as we have illustrated. The energy flow of the old pattern shows that the energy moves clockwise above the equator or the navel. Below the equator or the navel, the energy moves counter-clockwise, forming a figure "8", (the infinity symbol). Half is negative; half is positive. Fold the picture. The center moves to the bottom, the bottom meets the top, and the energy flow is altered. In a manner of speaking, what is occurring is that you are folding the directions of your energy and, at the same time, you are folding time and the dimensions within your physical body.

Your journey through the duality polarity of oppositional consciousness is how you created success and failure in third dimension. Through these opposing forces, you experienced and you created your lessons. In the No-Time and the Void, by rising above the conflict of duality that was ingrained in you, you now have the choice to break down the Wall of limitations through unconditional love of self and transcend. You are the One and only One who can initiate your change of consciousness from the polarity of duality to your Oneness of Consciousness. This is an integration of your multiple dimensional consciousness.

The conflict was ingrained in your body, in your DNA, in your biology, and through the process of conditioning. Your key to discernment between your Truth and the "trues" of the programs is accessed through your Feeling Center - your Heart and Solar Plexus Chakras. You cannot break through the Wall using your head. Thinking has nothing to do with it. Only through feeling from your heart and the integrated consciousness of your male, female, and your child-within can you break through the Wall. The energy and consciousness that breaks down and dissolves the Wall is unconditional love. That is, unconditional love without hooks, boundaries, manipulations, or controls. This means unconditional love!

You, and only you, can make that choice for yourself. You can choose to nurture the principle of unconditional love, to comprehend that your light is the knowledge within you, and to nourish your energy through self love...unconditionally. Or, you can simply choose again the fear consciousness that holds you in the duality of opposition, and be again and again surrounded by the Wall and caught in third dimension's recycled infinity.

The moment you choose to initiate, consciously and intentionally, the activation and process of your physical Thirteen Chakras, your body begins to release the density of the third dimension. Your light body is set free from the conditions, the emotional hooks, and the outcomes from either the past or the repetitious future. You now have new choices to create a new future in the No-Time and the Void.

As you have begun breaking through the Wall and the barriers of fear of the third dimensional limited perspectives, you will begin to feel all of your dimensions are coming together in your process of re-membering, re-calling and re-collecting yourself. This will take an enormous energy, or frequency shift, for your human body as you pass through the electromagnetic Wall of fear that has blocked the access to the multiple dimensions of your being. All of the dimensions have always been and are right now within you. As this occurs, time compacts. You are in the moment. You create from the present. Your consciousness expands. You are becoming multiple dimensional in the Now of the No-Time No Space.

To Be Or Not To Be,
Not To Be Is Impossible.
To Be is All.
Wei Chen

The Thirteen Chakra Open Template of Unlimited Consciousness and Creativity:

The movement of Creative Energy flows in all directions without restrictions.

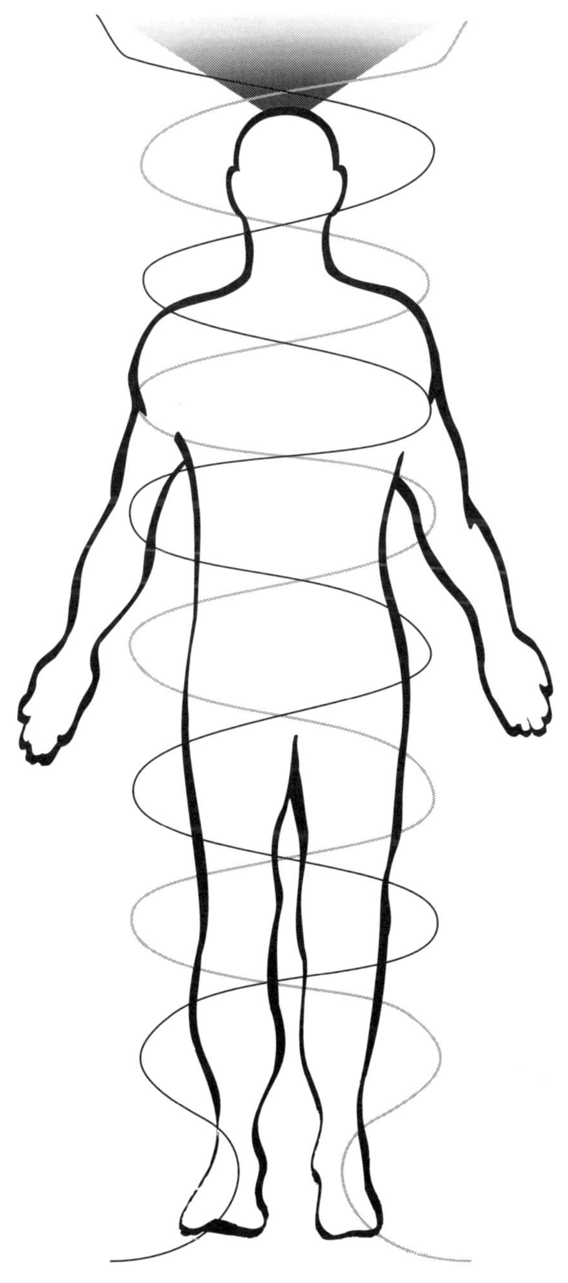

The Activation of the Thirteeen Chakras

Synergy and Synchronicity of the New Electromagnetic Fields and DNA Strands

Man's possession by inheritance,
His hereditary possession,
Is the soul, the whole consciousness,
At one with the Christ mind and
Constantly open to ideas from the One mind.

Metaphysical Bible Dictionary

Chapter 7
The Shift
The Activation of the Thirteen Chakras

The twelve faculties of man's divine mind are
Symbolized by the twelve disciples of Jesus Christ,
with their origin in the One Consciousness
Transfigured body.

Metaphysical Dictionary

Angels are the power hidden in the faculties and origins of man.

Ibn al-' Arabi the Murcian
Greatest Master of the Sufi
1165-1240 AD

In the transcension of your consciousness from the Seven Primary Chakras of energy to the Thirteen Chakras in your physical body, the creative process follows a path of partnership with the faculties of energy that correspond to the twelve divine disciples within you. The Thirteenth Chakra is your union of consciousness within you that symbolizes the consciousness of Jesus that is your Christed Consciousness as your Divine Being of Self in your physical Earth body.

The twelve astrological signs also represent aspects of your evolution to your Christed Consciousness. You can view your astrological chart as your journey through linear time similar to the Earth's journey as it rotates around the sun through each sign. Each sign, just as in duality, has aspects of oppositional consciousness under the sign in which you were born. You chose that sign with all its aspects as another avenue in your journey of multiplicity to gain more insight about yourself along your travels in your lifetimes.

Whatever sign you chose in a particular lifetime holds many keys to how you processed that linear frame of time under that sign. Your journey of consciousness is analogous to the relationship of the journey of the Earth's consciousness through each astrological sign and frame of time as it moves around the sun. Each sign has a consciousness as each frame of linear time does. You evolved through your astrological sign as well as the collective consciousness of the sign in which the Earth was evolving.

The significance of the disciples is that they represent aspects of you that are embodied in your consciousness whether you are aware of this connection or not. Their connection to Christ is the parallel to your connection of their aspects within you to your Christed Consciousness. They supported Christ with the energy of unconditional love as the aspects of your own discipleship within you will support you in unconditional love. The key is allowing yourself to comprehend that you are deserving of receiving unconditional love from yourself.

In the transcension of your conscious awareness, because of these divine aspects that are a part of you, you are energetically and consciously moving along your (higher) astrological path from duality to the unlimited and beyond.

As you ascend your consciousness you are remembering that there is nothing outside of you that is not an aspect of you. Everything in the physical world, regardless of the level of consciousness, is a part of you. Everything beyond the dimension of this physical world is also a part of you. In the process of your transcension, you are becoming the connection for yourself as well as the inter-link to the multiple dimensional levels of consciousness inside and outside of you.

The correlation between the expansion of your consciousness, and the expansion of the consciousness of the Earth itself, is occurring as a symmetry of a unified field of expanded awareness. As you, an individual, transcend your consciousness beyond the oppositional field of duality and its foundation of fear, the Earth also transcends.

The Earth, as a living being by divine agreement, is the place or location in the time continuum that provides the space for you and for everyone to participate on all the roads of discovery of Yourself. The Earth holds for you and for everyone the energy field in which you journey through the frequency and vibration of your consciousness at each particular linear time frame. The Earth is always conscious of this, even when you are not.

The Christed Consciousness was birthed over two thousand years ago. In this current millennium of the 2000's, the old grid pattern surrounding the Earth, which relates to the Seven Chakras of consciousness of recycled patterns and behaviors, is now breaking down. The breaking down of the grid is reflected by the transcension of consciousness within each and every one of you on this planet.

Your grid, or blueprint, is now beginning to open. It does not disappear, except that now it is here as a foundation of physicality for your creativity and your creations to have physical substance. This new grid is not fixed, but fluid and flexible, as is the creativity of your Higher Consciousness that is awakening. The concept, or the idea of the grid is to provide us with a sense of dimension and physicality.

This transcension is the universal shift of consciousness for you, everyone, and the Earth itself. The grid is shifting and opening as you are shifting to your Christed Consciousness. This is the synchronicity and synergy of the multiple dimensions of consciousness, inter-linked and connected as you become Who You Are.

By releasing yourself from the control and manipulation of the fears and the programs, you create the shift. As this occurs, the frequency and vibration of you, everyone, the Earth itself, and everything shifts. How long this takes is up to each and every one of you. Again, it was two thousand years ago since the Christed Consciousness was activated on this planet.

The question is, "Are you willing to expend another two thousand years of duality and living in the fears to create the shift?"

Your quest is, "Are you willing to let go of the fears and the illusions, right here, right now, and birth from within you the activation onto this physical planet of your Higher Consciousness from which to create your life and participate to your fullest?"

THE THIRTEEN CHAKRAS

Please review the Thirteen Chakra Chart, which includes the Zodiac sign, the discipleship, the colors, the symbols, the crystals, the essential oils and the consciousness relating to each Chakra.

First Chakra/Feet: Soul of Your Earth Body-Foundation

As you shift physically, electro-magnetically, and consciously from the Seven to the Thirteen Chakras, the First Chakra to activate is at the bottom of your feet. Consider the metaphor, when you "heal your soul", you begin to take a new stand for yourself.

This First Chakra represents the soul of your Earth-body. It is your new foundation of consciousness. The disciple that represents your new stand is Judas. Contrary to popular belief that he is the traitor, he is not. It took incredible courage and bravery on Judas's part to play out his role in the ascension of Jesus. Judas was the one who accepted the role of "betrayer" and acted out his role accordingly.

In the old consciousness, he represents the aspect of each of you whenever you betray yourself from being your Truth as you act out your role accordingly. This is not a judgment of what you do or have done. In the old paradigm of duality, you play out both the betrayer and the betrayed. What you learn about yourself from the experience is all that matters now. How you use that information is all that matters now. In the old pattern of this paradigm, the behavior represents the victim and the victimizer.

As you take your stand for yourself in your expanded consciousness, it requires courage, bravery, and your willingness to be vulnerable. It requires you to let go of any outside judgment of being either a betrayer or the betrayed, victim or victimizer of the old programmed behavior as you make your shift, just as Judas agreed to do. He played the part supporting Jesus as no one else could have done. He loved himself and Jesus unconditionally to play this role. In your transition you are required to love yourself unconditionally, no matter what the outside is trying to reflect back to you.

Initiating taking your stand for yourself also changes the dynamics of the old paradigm that everyone outside of you is your reflection. In the old paradigm of duality, it is true that they are your reflections. In the transcension of consciousness, being a reflection of yourself, or you being a reflection of someone else, is no longer pertinent to the dynamics of relationships.

As you go through the process of their activation, the consciousness of the energy field for the Thirteen Chakras is to see all of the aspects of your multiple dimensional selves as the reflection of yourself initially. The reflection of all of these aspects is what teaches you about Who You Are and all that you have experienced to learn about Yourself. Eventually there is no requirement for being a reflection as you ascend your consciousness.

Pisces, the Twelfth house, is aligned to the First Chakra of this newer system. Jesus was born in the Piscean Age. Jesus represents the rising above the emotions and the emotional hooks to the programming, as depicted in the metaphor of Him walking on the water. As you rise above the consciousness of duality's emotional hooks, particularly the "wanty-needy" low-based energy of being right or even wrong, you, in the same metaphoric sense, are ascending, or walking along your path above this low-based consciousness. It no longer holds you in a frequency or vibration of "wanty-needy", victim/victimizer consciousness.

Duality consciousness conditions you to participate in emotionally charged fields of energy repeatedly. These fields of energy are like mirrors. Like the trickster mirrors in a carnival, what was reflected back to you is that the outside was your reflection. In that venue, you were conditioned to be emotionally hooked to the outside of yourself.

The frequency and the vibration of this emotionally charged energy field held you stuck in the density of third dimension's grid. As you leave this old consciousness and stand for your Truth without having the emotional hooks to bind you in the grid pattern of third dimension, you begin to free yourself from the past.

In the activation of this First Chakra, you rise above the

emotions, and all the hooks of the programs to which you are attached, as you take your stand for yourself. Your feet become grounded to Earth, and yet, at the same time, your vibration and frequency increases and expands. Your polarity is changing and aligning. A new beginning, a new consciousness and a new multiple dimensional reality begins. You stand for your Truth and yourself. You are beginning to heal and align yourself with your soul in your physical body.

The multiple dimensional consciousness of your energy arises from your feet into your ankles. This is your stand.

Second Chakra/Ankles: Female/Male Energy Alignment

The Second Chakra to be activated is the ankles. In the old pattern the ankles represented not having sufficient support, whether it is emotional, financial, spiritual, personal, or all of the above. Whatever the issues of non-support that you manifested in your lives, these issues are emotionally connected to the old paradigm of separatism. The separatism consciousness, regardless of the non-support issues, is directly related to the separation of the male and female aspects within your physical body of consciousness.

The challenge in the frequency and vibrational grid of duality is to align the non-support issues of both the male and the female aspects within you. Because of all of your lives in the time continuum of either being male or female, and because these experiences are held within your body of consciousness as cellular memory, memorization, and sound, the density of third dimension does not provide a stable field of energy in which to release your issues. Due to the instability of this field, the male and female aspects of you could not simultaneously release their non-supportive issues from the consciousness held in your ankles. Duality supports you to be separate from within yourself. The dynamics of the density of the duality consciousness also makes it difficult to connect to all the layers of consciousness stored in the different parts and areas of your body relating to your male and female issues.

In the idea of "no support", confusion results from the

perspective of not only the male and female aspects of you, but from the child within you. When the child within you is silently and sometimes unconsciously held in a grid of non-support issues, the separation of consciousness within you is fragmented into another field of consciousness. Whether your issues and fears deal with the representation of the males outside of you, and/or the representation of the females outside of you, your manifested insecurities, are fears concerning support, which reflect your inner-male, inner-female and inner-child support issues of consciousness in the physicality of your ankles.

Consider for a moment all of the physical maladies of the feet and ankles. Physical manifestations of the non-support consciousness that are locked in your body appear as feet issues, ingrown toenails, bunions, fallen arches, broken bones, weak ankles, etc. Duality cannot provide a continuous energy field to allow for an alignment of your male, your female and your child-within to release these issues simultaneously, synergistically, and synchronisticly.

In the Thirteen Chakra System your male and female energies become aligned as you recognize that all support comes from within you. The old system conditions you that your support is outside of you. As you make the shift from the old consciousness, the energy of your consciousness also shifts, because you now comprehend that it is you who determines that you are supported. Supported first by yourself, the energy, then, that which emanates from you, drawing to you support from outside of yourself.

The difference is you are not emotionally hooked to either being or not being supported. In the dynamics of this field you become an attractor for support. You become supported because you support yourself. In this field there is no frequency or vibration for "wanty-needy", victim/victimizer consciousness or behavior.

This supportive energy can now come from family, friends, and associates. This consciousness of support occurs because you are in alignment with yourself. The frequency and vibration to draw to you those who do not support you shifts. There is no reason to draw to you any more those outside of you who do not support you. For those who do not support you are no longer magnetically drawn to you, because your field of magnetic energy does not attract them. Your male, female, and your child-within are aligned in supporting you.

Aquarius, the Eleventh House of the Zodiac, represents this Chakra. Eleven is a master number, which represents two symbols, a one and a one standing in alignment. Alignment means without opposition, without the polarity of the duality consciousness. Aquarius is the pure water-bearer, balancing out the emotions and the illusions of obstacles and opposition to the higher thought process of this air sign. You are in balance and not attached to the emotions that hooked you to the Duality Programs. In the alignment of your male and female standing as One Consciousness of your multiple dimensional self, which includes the child within you, your body becomes aligned in the integration process of your higher frequency and vibration in the physical, spiritual, divine mind and soul levels of yourself.

Thaddeus (Jude) is the disciple of the Second Chakra. He represents the balance of receiving the consciousness of your spirit through your female in alignment with your male consciousness of manifestation, in unity with the child-within. Through this balance and alignment of the male and female, a process of releasing the fears of non-support begins.

Thaddeus (Jude) is the faculty within you that signifies the elimination or release of fear from your male and female consciousness. Releasing his own fear and standing for his own Truth, Thaddeus traveled long distances teaching and healing. He had aligned himself with his own Christed Consciousness and was a disciple of Jesus. As the Patron Saint of Desperate Causes, he is the one to ask for help when all else fails. This aspect of the Thaddeus consciousness lies within you. At your most desperate moment, when all else fails, you will always find the Truth within yourself.

As this happens, you are now initiating the letting go of fear-based thoughts, conditions, ideas, and hidden consciousness that no longer serve you on any level, dimension, or realm of yourself. Your energy and consciousness of unconditional love begins to support you in this alignment of your male and female, embracing the child-within, supporting each other as One Body of

Consciousness. Fear of non-support begins to be eliminated. The idea of needing and wanting support from outside yourself releases from your ankles. You begin to stand, aligned within yourself, comprehending you are the source of your own support.

The consciousness of being alone and lonely also begins to be released from within you. You comprehend you are not alone. You have the support not only of yourself, but also of the Universal Consciousness of Oneness. Your energy and your consciousness are ascending up through your physical body.

Third Chakra/Knees: What You Stand For

The knees are your Third Chakra. Significantly, in the old system they represent the consciousness of being brought to your knees in the frequency and vibration of being controlled, manipulated, and invalidated. You and everyone on this planet, have experienced this consciousness in some lifetime or another, when you were not validated about an idea or creative concept that you had. Your idea may have felt as though it was coming from the depths of your creativity and your soul. Or it may have felt as if it was coming through you as an intuitive burst that you were sure would change your life if you could manifest it. The child of your many lifetimes has experienced these moments many times.

In these experiences in your time continuum, the frequency of duality set you up to be opposed. In the lifetimes you could not overcome the opposition through the Judgment Program, you failed from a third dimensional perspective. The Lack Program determined that you did not have what it takes. And through the Take-Away Program, the manifestation of your idea was taken away, and it did not happen.

In the lifetimes that you could overcome the opposition, you manifested your idea. But it is always temporary because the consciousness of duality has the emotional stress or hook of when the Take-Away Program will manifest itself. Without a sense of security and support, in a metaphoric sense, you were brought to your knees when you did not comprehend that your idea or your burst of intuitive creativity had a value.

All of your experiences that represent your power being taken away from you, whether from the male, the female, or the child within you, are held within the consciousness of your knees. Look at all the physical issues surrounding the knees: knee replacements, torn cartilage, arthritis, joint issues, etc. Regardless of the treatment, or even a replacement, the consciousness of having your power taken away still remains embedded in your knees. You cannot "cure" your consciousness. Coming to consciousness is becoming aware of yourself on all the levels of consciousness in which you participate. You then have chosen to retain or release the consciousness that no longer serves or benefits you. You've gotten the lesson!

In the alignment of the male/female/child-within through your memories, memorizations and sounds, you can choose to release the consciousness of opposition from your time continuum. In doing so you release from your knees the fears that previously prevented you from creating *what you stand for* in your life.

Fear, though you "think" it is coming from an outside source, is within you. It is your conditioned, fear-based consciousness that brought you to your knees in all of your lifetimes. In the ascension of your consciousness detaching from the programs of Judgment, Lack and Take-Away, you are the one person who is now the representative of *what you stand for*.

This does not mean that *what you stand for* must be in opposition to someone else. In the Universal Consciousness of Oneness there is space for everyone to stand for themselves. This field of energy does not hold a frequency or vibration for opposition, war, or harm. There is no requirement for this behavior.

It may appear that this is a simplistic approach, and it is. Cleared consciousness is simple. Consciousness based on fear is complicated because of the emotional attachments and hooks. The fear is about being wrong or invalidated.

Simon is the disciple of the Third Chakra. He was viewed as a typical man with Earthly emotional highs and lows. His ordinary life can be seen as a process, like our own, in the ascension to his Higher or Christed Consciousness. Simon represents overcoming the fear and bringing your idea into substance.This is called manifestation with clarity. This manifestation results from standing firmly in the faith that your ideas are grounded in the spiritual principles, and through the integration of consciousness of your male, female and child-within. You are supported from a foundation cleared from the fears at your soul level in your physical body. Get up off your knees physically, and metaphorically, and stand for Yourself and your ideas.

Capricorn, the Tenth house, represents the authorship of your ideas. Ten represents the idea of one, numerically new beginnings. Your new beginnings are initiated when you have absolute faith in yourself, that you validate yourself and your creative ideas. You initiate new beginnings in your life, each day, by allowing new ideas to come through you.

You determine which idea you manifest. Instant manifestation is the instant you select which of your inspired ideas you choose to bring through into your physical world. The linear frame of time has nothing to do with it when you live in the present moment. Only in the present moment are you *what you stand for*. Your knees become as flexible as your life becomes. Your energy and your consciousness are rising.

Fourth Chakra/Hips and Upper Legs: Passion and Commitment

The disciple Thomas was known as Doubting Thomas, a man not willing to believe unless he could see it physically. His ultimate test came when Jesus died and was resurrected into a higher state of consciousness. When he understood that Jesus' death represented the death of old consciousness in the physical body and his resurrection represented the birth of the Christed Consciousness in the physical body on the Earth plane, he stopped doubting.

As the representative of the Fourth Chakra, Thomas symbolizes the transition from the lower to higher consciousness, and the connection between your higher understanding and your divine will. In this shift from doubt to trust, the male and female aspects of yourself become aligned. You understand the "trusting" of your

Higher Self and you see the significance of your divine will in your creative process. Your hips and upper legs are the region that embodies this alignment. You are beginning to stand for yourself and your Truth without doubt.,

You have joined forces with yourself. In that energy field of divine will you are balanced and cannot be forced out of alignment within yourself. At this point you have expanded your consciousness too far to go back. Your male and female cannot be separated again. They are inter-linked and inter-connected as you are ascending and integrating your many levels of consciousness. Making your passionate commitment to yourself continues your process of transcension of consciousness.

By understanding and comprehending that there is this connection between your female spirit (feeling) and your physical male body (activity), you realize the importance of aligning these twin aspects of yourself. This does not mean the alignment is based on duality. The physical alignment, located in your hips and upper legs, is the divine will union of your female creative passion with your male creative action. This activity of your energy field focuses your divine will from the unification of your male and female without the tumultuous energy of your ego's manipulating willfulness.

Sagittarius, the archer, the Ninth house, projects the ideas of your divine will from this male/female unity of your Higher Consciousness. Through this divine will, there is no risk that your life and your ideas are not worthy of validation. In faith, you completely comprehend that all your ideas previously buried within you because of your fears, can now be resurrected and manifested through your passion and commitment to yourself.

In this Chakra, by releasing your fears you choose to manifest which ideas you have that honor your life and your ideas. In your shift of focused consciousness, your understanding and comprehension of your divine will will empower you. You validate yourself. You are resurrecting and rebirthing the divine will energy through this union and unity. You realize your transcension into empowerment is through your divine will. Sagittarius represents the number Nine. Numerically this is the idea of God-reality. Metaphorically God-reality is a completion of the old consciousness. Releasing ego's willfulness raises your frequency and vibration into your new field of divine will consciousness. You are your God-reality. No one else can make God real for you. You are God.

Fifth Chakra/Reproductive Organs: Creativity

The Generative, or sexual Chakra is the source of your creativity. The important key in your creative process is to completely comprehend that what you create and manifest in your life "outside" of you is generated from your creative Chakra based upon the foundation of what you believe. Be it fear or clear, your creative process belongs to you and no one else. As your new Chakra System unfolds, your creativity becomes empowered because you are being the cause without all those fears of the Judgment, Lack, and Take-Away Programs. Matthew is the disciple which represents the gift or gratuity of the God-creativeness within you. Matthew is your faculty, which uplifts your creativity through your divine will through your divine mind.

Your creativity is your gift created from your Higher Consciousness consciously, and brings about the physical manifestations of what you require, desire, and absolutely deserve to create for yourself. Being gratuitous to yourself in all that you create in your life means you are creating clearly without fear and without the concept of "not-deserving." You are rising above the emotional hooks of the Judgment, Lack, and Take-Away Programs. You have no requirement to create your life within the restrictions and boundaries of these Duality Programs. The requirements you have are only concerned with you being absolutely clear about who, what, and where you put the focus of your creativity. Standing in the energetic center of your divine will and your divine mind is standing in the core of your creative empowerment.

Matthew was a tax collector, or someone to be feared. He was in a position of power over others, a symbol of control and manipulation. As the representative of the Fifth Chakra, Matthew signifies surrendering the old ideas and conditions of the lower consciousness. When you surrender the fear and the past, metaphorically, Matthew is the connection to your higher mind and divine thought process. This enables you to manifest your creativity in ways that best serve and honor your life. You are no longer creating from a foundation of fear. Fear, like a parasite, feeds off your energy. Like a parasite, fear drains your life-force. When the fear is so overwhelming, you can become paralyzed. Energetically, physically, and spiritually, you are immobile.

Not only are you immobile, but you are caught in a consciousness grid of self-created recycled patterns and behaviors. In this grid of fear, your reproductive creativity, regardless of linear time, produces conditions and situations in which your patterns and behaviors are imprinted by the Judgment, Lack, and Take-Away Programs. Through the release of these imprints in your Creative Chakra, only you, by your choice in the consciousness of your divine will and divine mind, erase these imprints. There is no requirement to re-create through your old patterns and behaviors of fear, unless you feel you require another interaction into a particular lesson.

As you activate this Fifth Chakra of divine will and divine mind, you comprehend that your creativity and your creative process are founded upon universal unconditional love for your self. You are now comprehending, as you ascend the focus of the energy of your divine will and your divine mind through your physical body of consciousness, that the first relationship that you have on this planet Earth or anywhere in your time continuum is with your self.

When you deny this relationship and stay separated from yourself, you deny the magnificence of your creativity. Your creativity is your purpose for being on this planet. Any and all facets of your purposes cannot be manifested until you are clear in your divine mind that your creativity is the foundation of your manifestations.

What you manifest in your life is where you are...consciously or unconsciously. What you manifest into your life is clearly defined by the relationship that you have with your self, at whatever level or levels of awareness you have about yourself. The source of your creativity, when you transcend from the ego and the grid of duality, is your divine mind through divine will of unlimited potentials, possibilities, and manifestations. In this field of consciousness your creative process is limitless. You are your own inter-link and the connection to the Universal Consciousness of Oneness' Law of Creative Empowerment. You are the Creator, the creativity, and the creation.

Your relationships outside of you become stronger and your real possessions are multiplied. Abundance and prosperity abound. They do so because you are not limiting your Self. Your self-creativity through the Universal Law of Attraction is now based on your self-consciousness founded on self-love and self-worth. This self-love and self-worth consciously energize your creativity, your creative process, and your self-created manifestations.

This Fifth Chakra of creativity is aligned with Scorpio, the Eighth House. The eight symbolically represents your break through the Block Wall. This fear-based version of infinity impelled you to participate through the controlling and manipulative energy of duality in your time continuum. Now this fear-based version no longer holds you in this grid of emotional attachments that impacted your creative process with cycles of the Judgment, Lack, and Take-Away Programs.

Remember when you created something that was so "good" you could hardly believe it was true? Remember when you feared the ax would fall to take it away? Now remember that you created both the "it was so good" and the "ax" to cut yourself off from the good. Now be clear again, and remember that you are the Creator, the creativity, and the creation.

As you release the fears that were ingrained in your creative process in your Now, you release them from your time continuum at your cellular level. There is no value in storing fear in your body anywhere.

Five, in numerology, represents wisdom. Your divine wisdom guides your creativity in synchronicity with your divine mind. The creative process belongs to you. Through conscious creativity the empowerment and force of your energy rises in your physical body, created by you.

Sixth Chakra/Solar Plexus: The Child-Within, Feeling Center, Balance, and Understanding

Your solar plexus is the child-within you. It represents all the children within you and your time continuum of experiences. Whether you were conscious or not, these experiences are the opportunities to learn about yourself and your participation. They are your gift to yourself to overcome your fears and illusions. Without judging yourself anymore, you will come to understand and comprehend that all of these experiences even as the child(ren) were created by you to learn about yourself along your journeys.

As you allow your child to begin to integrate into a Unified Field of Consciousness, you begin to heal all those children from all of your lifetimes. You are activating the balance at your quantum cellular level of healing within your time continuum of experiences in your intelligence. You are becoming One with your child(ren).

James, a half brother of Jesus, at first did not believe in him or his teachings. He was influenced by the opinions of others. He was said to have thought that Jesus was out of his mind. It was after the resurrection of Jesus to his Higher Consciousness that James became a believer in the Christed Consciousness within himself.

James is your faculty in your Higher Consciousness that represents your higher ability to discern between the "true" of the old paradigm and the Truth within your Higher Consciousness. The old paradigm of your ego's judgment no longer serves the child or you within your adult physical body. Through the discernment of your divine mind in your intelligence, you empower yourself to make clear choices through the union of your female (spirit) and your male (physical) body in alignment with the child within you.

With your child you see life with newness. You experience life as the child does when he or she is discovering something new for the first time. Your consciousness and your energy are not jaded and limited by the fears. There is no requirement to place the focus of your energy with concerns of being rejected or abandoned. Not only will rejection and abandonment be released from your consciousness, you will no longer be burdened by the fears of not being validated.

As you unify with your child to participate with you in your adult body now, you heal the child within you. Your child(ren) become a resource within your consciousness from which to draw upon your experiences from your cellular memory, memorization, and sound associated with the experiences.

Your child's resource of information assists you to understand and comprehend how you participated in your lifetimes as the child. You will discover and then comprehend that each of your adults within your time continuum was affected by the experiences, whether an illusion or the Truth, of the child(ren) within you. You will comprehend that your child was never separated from you. You will comprehend that your child is an active participant in your adult life, whether you accept or deny this.

The consciousness of your child is integral to the consciousness of your creativity and behavior in your adult life. Intellectually, you may "think" your child does not impact your life as you psychologically process the healing of your child's experiences and fears through the logic of your computer-brain. You can intellectualize the fears and the experiences through your computer-brain. You cannot, however, intellectualize them out of your body, either as a child or an adult. You do it through the release of cellular memory, memorization, and sound, and the emotional attachments to the experiences from your ego's perspective.

Your intelligence is your real brain of consciousness. Through this divine brain you can release your child(ren) and your adult(s) from the fears and the experiences resulting from the fears. Your brain is a complex computer controlled by your ego that perceives your life as complex and fearful. Your intelligence is your divine mind inter-linked to your divine child.

This divine mind/brain is a resource of your child(ren)'s history within you. With discernment as your key to unlocking your history, you discover that the source of your participation has been encompassed by fear. In your intelligence you feel the difference between the fears that manipulated you in the past and in your clarity now that you choose how you participate in your life going forward. Always trust your feelings in your intelligence.

Your intelligence, your child within you, will always discern your Truth. Your brain will always decide which Fear Program in which to participate. Your child-within is also a Source of your empowerment. Releasing your child consciously from the perceptions and the illusions of the fear, releases you as the adult from this old consciousness.

As the adult, you move beyond the illusional criteria upon which your actions, behaviors, and participations were unconsciously based. You no longer separate your adult self from your child self. In your expanded awareness of your inter-link and your connection to your child(ren) within you, you are becoming as One.

You realize and recognize the child within you has been your teacher all along the journeys in your time continuum. Now your adult is the student discovering and learning to hold and be the physical energy on this Earth plane of your Higher Consciousness. Your divine mind, your divine will, and the divine wisdom of each are becoming integrated within you.

Your dynamic energy field of your intelligence is a unifying balance of your male, your female, and your child-within. Discernment is the key to this unification. Discernment is your clarity to choose what honors you or not. The energy and consciousness of judgment has no place or value in your expanded consciousness of discernment.

You comprehend what is right for you. You comprehend what is your Truth. And you comprehend where to focus your energy. Comprehension, your knowing and understanding in balance and focus, is your discernment. Discernment is empowerment. You cannot give your power away, or have it taken away, because you comprehend that you are being the cause of everything in your life. In discernment you choose with whom, where, and why you opt to participate or not. Discernment is the Higher Consciousness within your intelligence. Again, your intelligence is your divine mind. It does not "think" through the use of logic and intellect. It is your intellect and your intelligence. Logic may be true. The intelligence and intellect in your body is your Truth.

Your child is an active participant in your creativity and manifestations. Through this participation you create a balanced and productive life. You no longer have room to hold the energy of a wounded child in your adult body. Your child is healed and empowered, rebirthed from this union of your healed male and healed female within you. You are becoming One.

Libra, the Seventh House, the Scales of Balance, is significant to this balance of the male/female/child-within. In this balance, there is no requirement to go back through the old Seven Chakra System of duality and the recycling of the fear-based programs. In this place of the No-Time and No-Space you have a choice. You can choose to recycle again through the old system. Or, you can choose to move forward and continue to ascend your consciousness.

Now you comprehend with your divine intellect that it is up to you to empower yourself. You are the one that balances your life. No one outside of you can bring you balance. You are the intelligence. This intelligence is your Truth. You cannot be manipulated by the fears again. Your intelligence feels. Discernment is your key to choice. Your choice is what determines your process and your participation. You comprehend because you feel. You feel because it is your Truth. Your Truth is your energy and consciousness of balance. When your child within your intelligence is balanced, secure in Truth, so are you as the adult. You are One in Balance and Truth.

In numerology, six represents balance. The male and the female, the yin and the yang, are balanced within a circle. The circle represents the connection of the child-within encircled in a balanced relationship with the male and female within you.

Seventh Chakra/Diaphragm: Information Assimilation (Food of Consciousness)

The diaphragm is the site within you which inspires your body with your Prana or higher breath of consciousness. This higher breath of energy breathes life into the realm of your imagination and creativity. Your divine breath energizes your imagination and creativity. This breath breathes a higher frequency and vibration into the essence of your creativity in your Creative Chakra. The disciple Nathanael/Bartholomew represents your divine imagination inspired by your higher breath of consciousness. Jesus called him ." .an Israelite indeed, in whom is no guile...". In this description, Jesus describes Nathanael/Bartholomew as being trustworthy and without deceit. Jesus continues to say that." Nathanael/Bartholomew) will see heaven opened, and the angels of God ascending and descending upon the Son of man." He is describing the ascension of Nathanael/Bartholomew's consciousness descending or grounding into his physical body. In the descending or grounding of the Higher Consciousness into the physical body, the higher breath of consciousness is activated and inspires the creative process of your life.

Breathing from your diaphragm infuses divine breath into each of the cells of your body. Your cells are inspired to release their knowledge of you from the deepest levels of your consciousness. In these levels are your history and experiences beyond your third dimensional lifetimes.

These levels of consciousness and experiences in your time continuum will inspire you to both know and acknowledge that you have indeed experienced and participated in dimensions and realms of consciousness where you are a Master. If this were not so, you would not be reading this. For something or anything to come into the physicality of third dimension, it is first spoken or written. Whether spoken or written, it is then infused with breath to bring the concept into context.

Breathing the vibration and frequency of your divine breath into your life on this planet shifts the energy within the breath of life in this dimension. As you expand your consciousness from these levels, so is the breath of your consciousness expanded. The breath of your consciousness, an expanded band of energy, flows from within you. It can be felt. Just as the expanded field of your aura is felt emanating from your body, so too can this field of energy, your divine breath, be felt.

You are recognizing that you are activating another level of your multiple dimensional self. What words you speak, what form of thought, what concept of your imagination you speak now into the physical is felt and inspired outside of you by you from the essence and life force of your divine breath. As a Master, the essence of your life force breathes the example of Mastery to others.

In the breath or field of consciousness of a Master, there is no place for a frequency and vibration of duality and opposition. Fear is neither a concept nor a reality. There is no requirement to speak a sound or word which vibrates a frequency of fear regardless of language.

The breath of your Higher Consciousness is not in any realm, dimension, or place outside of you. It is a deeper level of your being. Infusing this Higher Consciousness of your breath into your creativity becomes your creation. You are the Creator, the creativity, and the creation.

You are remembering now that what you breathe into your life will inspire your creativity and your manifestations. Or, if you continue to participate in the consciousness of duality, you will at some point allow your life force to be sucked out of you by some outside source. Illnesses relating to breathing issues in your body are not just physical. They are emotional issues,attached to an outside source stored in your unconsciousness, which appear as though your breath is being sucked out of you. You are not breathing your life to its fullest. These illnesses are your body's physical manifestations created from the fears of not being able to fully breathe Life into your life.

You unconsciously and unwittingly allow your breath to be sucked from your body. Breathing from your Higher Consciousness enfolds you in an energy field emanating from the Mastery Consciousness within you. A Master is not affected by the outside or by the illusion of the fears. The consciousness of the Master is concerned with either being neither a cause nor an effect. A Master is.

Virgo, the Sixth House, represents the purity of your imagination that is breathed into life through your Higher Consciousness. In simple terms, the purity is Virginal, which simply means without the contaminating breath of fear. Six, numerically representing balance, is the divine balance in the frequency and vibration of your physical body with the divine breath of your diaphragm. Your body and your breath are as One. You breathe with your Higher Consciousness. Fear no longer controls the breath (energy) of your life. You breathe your body into a higher vibration and frequency of consciousness as you transcend.

Eighth Chakra/Heart: Feeling Center

The disciple John symbolizes the Heart Chakra. The only Apostle present at the Crucifixion, it was to him that Jesus entrusted the love and protection of His beloved mother. Also known as John the Baptist, baptism represents the releasing of the old consciousness and fear. It is through the Heart Chakra that the fear consciousness is released and unconditional love evolves. John is the representative faculty of your Truth residing in the energy field of unconditional love within your heart. This faculty is the embodiment of your spiritual Truth that is guided by the divine intellect of your heart. As previously expressed, your Heart Chakra aligned with your intelligence is your Feeling Center. This center of feeling emits a field of unconditional love from within your heart in unison with your child-within.

In the frequency and vibration of unconditional love, only your Truth can be felt and expressed. Your Truth becomes the inspiration for your creativity. Your Truth becomes the inspired force or energy that empowers your actions and behaviors.

The energy of your Feeling Center has an unlimited capacity to experience the essence of your creative abilities. In written form, there really are no descriptive adjectives that define this unlimited capacity for living your life, standing in your Truth, and creating and manifesting from that Truth in third dimensional terms. Third dimensional language is limited by perceptions and illusions and their attachments to the fears.

Putting your energy and your consciousness of unconditional love into the physical embodiment of all of your creative ideas releases the restrictions and confinements of third dimension's limited capacity for creation. The consciousness of your heart in this Thirteen Chakra System is the Unlimited Consciousness of Oneness. This energy does not delineate differences as oppositional. It honors the differences as unique but not separate.

Your Heart Chakra of unconditional love and Truth is not only a conduit for you to live and create from the higher realms of your consciousness, it is also a conduit for you to connect and inter-link to the higher realms of consciousness on other dimensions without any fear. Though these dimensions are different, they are not separate from you.

The band of frequency of your Heart Chakra acts as both a transmitter and a receiver of unconditional love. You transmit the energy of unconditional love from within you. You also become a receiver of unconditional love, not only on this Earth plane, but you become a receptacle to accept unconditional love from other realms and dimensions. As a receiver, you become a conduit. You become a channel for angels, guides, soul groups and other beings outside of the Earth plane.

As you become aware that your Truth has many levels within your multiple dimensional consciousness, you become conscious that many levels of Truth abound within the structures of other dimensions and realms outside of your limited third dimensional perspectives. Universal Truth is the Oneness of Consciousness that allows for the differences of Truth within and between the dimensions.

Your Feeling Center is the heart of your feelings. The dynamics of this field does not provide a space in which fear can have life. The consciousness of your Heart Chakra, unconditional love, guides your intelligence, your real brain, through the creativity, actions, and manifestations of your newer Fifth Creative Chakra.

From your center of feeling, you are becoming at-onement with your self as the Creator, creativity and creation of your life. In this field of frequency and vibration there is no reason, excuse or logic to deny yourself Who You Are, as a perfect divine being.

In this alignment of consciousness your female, guided by your innate and inherent intuition, inspires your male to manifest into your physical world the idea of your creativity. The connection and the interaction of your male and female flows in the energy of unconditional love through your heart in unity with your intelligence. You are living and creating through the frequency, vibration, intelligence, and intellect of your divine Feeling Center. The band of conscious communication receiving through your left (female) hand and connecting to your right (male) hand produces your inspired creative idea into a physical reality. You are manifesting your life without the fear of Judgment, Lack, and Take-Away from yourself.

The frequency and vibrational consciousness of third dimension is separation. In the field of your Feeling Center your male and your female are in a proactive, unified, intentional consciousness to manifest. In this field the physicality of the female is integrated within the physicality of the male body, unlike in third dimension.

In third dimension, the physicality and consciousness of everyone's body is male energy. The female is separated as if a different entity and consciousness, not an actual integral part of the physicality of the male body of consciousness. In third dimension, the male body of consciousness is the energy of opposition and separation. In this consciousness, a harmonious unity of your male and female consciousness to be or stay aligned is almost impossible to sustain.

In your Feeling Center, in the vibration and frequency of unconditional love in your Heart Chakra, your female is birthed onto this Earth into your physical body. She is your spirit, your intuition, and your inspiration. Your female has life. She has breath and she has voice in both your physical body and your physical world.

Leo, the Fifth House, signifies the ruler of fire and passion. When you have passion in your heart without fear, there are no obstacles to your creativity and your abilities to manifest what is in your heart. Your heart is the center of your Lifeing. Where you direct the consciousness of your heart's passion, you create your Truth. Your Truth is always in your heart.

Five numerically embodies wisdom. With the wisdom of your intuition and the creative alignment of your male, female, and child passionately embracing life in unconditional love, you live your Truth. You continue to ascend your consciousness without the fear of restrictions and limitations. This is not a dream or an illusion. You are creating a new reality for yourself, your life and for your world.

Ninth Chakra/Nervous System: Conscious Integration

The Ninth Chakra is your nervous system and your spinal column. These systems metaphorically embody the Tree of Life within you. Your nervous system is your messaging system. Your spinal column is imprinted with your Akashic Records, your entire history throughout your personal time continuum. Your historical information is imprinted on each disk, and is collectively known as your Asashic Records.

Through these systems, your body receives information, whether you are conscious of it or not. Whether you are processing this information through your third dimensional ego or your Higher Self, depends upon where you are emotionally and consciously in your time continuum.

When you are in a cycle of repeated behaviors and actions, regardless of your linear age, you are still processing this information from an age or stage in your life in which you are emotionally and energetically stuck. To release yourself from that place and time of this recycled consciousness, you realize you are required to rise above emotional attachments to that issue. It is time to evaluate and discern what the message you are receiving is really communicating to you. In the message is the core issue, underneath the emotional energy of the experience.

As you are ascending your consciousness into this higher vibrational field of your nervous system and your spinal column, you become physically calmer and detached from the emotions and the energetic hooks to the issues. In this state of calmness you can feel, see, and evaluate the messages as pure information that helps you overcome your emotional attachments.

Your nervous system is the conduit in which the vibration and frequency of your Higher Consciousness assists you in evaluating and discerning the Truth of your participation in experiences you created in your linear frames of times. The experiences are your lessons you required to learn about yourself and bring you to your place of Higher Consciousness in the Now.

Your nervous system becomes calmer. In this field of internal calmness, your outside life becomes calmer. You do not require yourself to process through nervous upheavals of the emotional issues or their behaviors and actions. Your unconscious becomes conscious.

As your awareness expands, the messages that no longer are pertinent to living a life in a lower vibrational field of consciousness are released. Since your energy is no longer embroiled or hooked into the lower vibrational fields of information, you are accessing not only the higher vibrational messages and information within you, you now are physically and consciously open to receive the higher vibrational frequencies of consciousness outside of you, not only on this planet, but outside the dimensional realms of third dimension.

Your nervous system, itself, is functioning at a higher vibrational frequency, above the fears of third dimension. Your nervous energy is calmer, more productive, and intuitive. You are now feeling the higher realms of vibrational frequency throughout your physical body, because your nervous system is in tune with these higher frequencies of consciousness.

In your spinal column you can access your Akashic records, which is the history of yourself that is stored on your discs. Without the fear or stress of the physicality of emotional releases of your issues at your cellular level, you can access your history of your time continuum from a "what-so" or "just is" perspective. You have risen above the emotional attachments to your issues. Your Akashic Records provide you with the historical accounts of your lifetimes not just on the Earth plane, but from the other dimensions and realms in which you have participated.

In those Records are your experiences as the Master that was discussed previously in this chapter. In this higher vibrational frequency of consciousness, there is no requirement for you to be fearful of this information. You are already the experience. Now use this information to benefit you in this lifetime.

You are the source as well as your own resource. The Higher

Consciousness of your nervous system illuminates your information, so there is no fear in the messages you received from your body. The information, regardless of the sensation, is to make you aware that something physically, spiritually, emotionally, and/or consciously is going on in a particular area of your body. This area is requiring your attention, your focus, and your consciousness. Your body is telling you something. In this higher vibrational frequency of consciousness, your intuition will tell you what it is. Listen and learn about your Self.

Your Akashic Records only require your attention as you choose to access the information at will. When you feel you are requiring to know about yourself, choose a particular area of your spinal column or a specific disc, direct your Higher Consciousness to that place, and allow yourself to receive the information. The information is you being informed about your Self. There is no one outside of you that knows more or has the resource of information about You than you.

In the higher vibrational frequency of your consciousness, you can neither deny the information about yourself nor deny that you are the information itself. You are now accessing and connecting to more levels of your multiple dimensional Self.

This Ninth Chakra, the nervous system, is your activation of your conscious integration, within your physical body, of your higher fields of information accessed because of its higher levels of vibrations and frequencies. During this integration, the strength of your Truth is felt throughout your entire body. Your nervous system is empowered to communicate the messages of your Truth to every cell in your body without the fear, energy, or consciousness of Judgment, Lack, and Take-Away.

You have the strength and the courage of your Truth to stand for your Self, by your Self, and with your Self. You are empowered with your "nerves of Truth." Your body emanates a consciousness of strength, not to be confused with your ego's idea of strength as control and manipulation. There is no strength in control and manipulation, only pain. There is no strength in pain no matter how much pain your ego says you can endure. Spiritual strength has no requirement for endurance. You just are strength because of your Truth.

James, the disciple of the Ninth Chakra, was the half-brother of Jesus. He was the first of the twelve disciples whose life ended as a martyr. The lesson in his life and death is that he had the spiritual strength to stand for his Truth. This doesn't mean that standing for your Truth requires you to die physically. It represents the death of the old consciousness. James represents the divine order of your strength which is inexhaustible when you live through your Truth. This is the strength which emanates from the conscious integration of order within your physical body through your divine mind, which is the intelligence and the intellect of your Higher Consciousness. In third dimension the emotional consciousness of fear has no order. It is disorder automatically.

Cancer, the Fourth House, represents the water electrically charged with the Higher Consciousness of your Ninth Chakra, your nervous system. Numerically it is a four, metaphorically representing your Now. The Now is your dimensional field of consciousness of the No-Time and the No Space. In this field, you are detached from the emotional issues and agendas of the past. In the Now, you are the observer.

As the observer, you see through the illusions of the emotional third dimensional issues. You have risen above the low-based frequencies of the emotional hooks. You are detached. You have no doubt about yourself. You know you are your strength. You comprehend your strength is your Truth. Now you can begin to speak your Truth.

Tenth Chakra/Throat: Communication

Philip is the disciple who represents the Throat Chakra. He demonstrated his power through the spiritual word, which he manifested in speech. As an evangelist and Bishop, he founded the Church of Glastonbury in Britain to teach the word of High Consciousness. Through the Throat Chakra your words will either empower or limit you.

Philip represents the power and strength of your words when

spoken from the frequency and vibration of your Higher Consciousness. He represents the power or the vital force, which carries the spiritual frequency or vibration of your Truth. The physical tones from within your body now emanate at a higher vibratory frequency. Your frequency is felt as an emanation of lightness. The frequency is no longer a dense vibration of fear. The sounds or tones of your frequencies from within your physical body are at-onement with each other. You are more harmonious within the frequencies of your multiple dimensional levels of consciousness. With life more harmonious inside of you, the life outside of you is more harmonious.

Now living in the higher vibrational frequencies of your consciousness, the words you speak inspire and empower your life. There are no reasons for you to speak words that do not honor you or your life. The idea of speaking self-sabotaging words, whether conscious or not, is irrelevant. In this higher vibrational field of your consciousness you speak the words and the language that support your Truth as a Creator, in the creative process of your creation. You would have no requirement to speak words that invalidate your Truth. When speaking this new vocabulary of your Higher Consciousness, there is no requirement to speak words that dishonor anyone else. Your words do not contain the tones or vibrational frequencies of opposition. When you speak your Truth without opposition you are standing firmly and balanced in your life. Your words are the sounds of your music, centered in harmony. Your words are harmonious to you and to those with whom you speak. When your words are spoken from the lower-based frequencies of consciousness, you are only in opposition to yourself. Any opposition you encounter outside of yourself is to hear that the discord is within you.

As you allow your thoughts and spoken words to be inspired from this higher level of your consciousness, the frequency and vibration of your life force changes. Your creative energy becomes enhanced to a more expanded level of productivity. Your productivity is not hampered by self-inflicted words and sounds of sabotage. When your words speak from a higher level of manifestation consciousness, you manifest a higher level of consciousness into your life. The manifestations of your creativity are conceived for yourself on requirement, desiring, and comprehending that you deserve the best life for yourself. You speak your Truth without ego or denial that you are deserving. When you speak your Truth, not only do you listen to yourself on all the levels of your consciousness, you feel it. When you speak your Truth, others outside of you hear it and feel it. And, when you speak your Truth, your vibration and frequency is both heard and felt on the other dimensions and realms. And when you speak your Truth to these other dimensions and realms, such as the angels, guides, and soul groups, they can assist you more easily because, in the frequency and vibration of your Truth, you are clear about what you are asking of them. You are not confused, and neither are they, about your requests. Every level and dimension in which you participate hears you clearly. When those outside of you on this Earth plane do not agree with your Truth, it does not matter. You are not emotionally attached to convincing or changing their views. You can agree to disagree without being or living in the lower vibrational frequencies of opposition. You no longer are involved in the consciousness of having to be right. Your Truth is you being right for yourself.

In this higher vibration/frequency of consciousness through your sound and spoken word, you no longer have the voice to resonate the vibrational energy of self-sabotage, self-criticism, and self-deficiency. You have changed your tune, or the frequency, of your vibration. You speak the words that support the meaning of your life. You have the strength and the empowerment to speak the words that mean your Truth, and to stand for your words of Truth that mean something to you. You are the only means to your Truth.

The Tenth Chakra is Gemini, the communicator, in the Third House. Gemini, the sign of the twins, portrays speaking your Truth with the balance of your male and female who are no longer in opposition to each other. Neither do you speak words of opposition to the child within you. The three represents your male, your female, and your child-within speaking harmoniously as one voice, not three separate facets of your consciousness. You are a vocal triad of Truth speaking from your heart with a voice that is unified through the conscious integration of your Truth. You are strong and empowered. You have the choice and the voice to speak your Truth. Your tones, sounds, and words are uplifted and raised by the higher vibrational frequency of your new consciousness.

Eleventh Chakra/The Third Eye: The Vision Center

Andrew is the disciple of your Vision Center. Through the insight of his Higher Consciousness, he brought his brother Simon to know Jesus as the representative of the Christed Consciousness. Your Christed consciousness expands your physical vision of awareness beyond the limitations of third dimension.

Your Vision Center provides you with the visual substance to see the possibilities and potentials of your creativity, before you actually manifest them into your physical world. Your Vision Center, pulsating in tune with the higher vibrational field of your consciousness, produces visual special effects. These special effects are produced so you can see what you desire to create in your life and what it requires to create it.

In the density of the lower vibrational field of third dimension, how could you see the vision of your possibilities and potentialities? The density of that frequency does not allow you to hold a vision of Higher Consciousness for an extended period of linear time. The density of third dimension limits not only the visions for yourself, but it limits the range of your visions.

Your intuition is the consciousness that energizes the frequency of your Vision Center. When your intuition is connected to your vision and inter-linked to your Creative Chakra and your creativity is founded upon the Truth of your passion for the creative process, you become unlimited in what you can create for yourself.

Your intuition provides the insight for the process of your creative ideas. Your intuition gives stability to your vision. Your heart provides the feeling to comprehend that you are creating from your Truth. Seeing from your vision center and trusting your intuition, you will know if your idea is based upon your Truth. Your Vision Center is your Higher Consciousness showing you what is the Truth for you.

Your Vision Center shows you that you, indeed, have the potential to create and manifest at your highest vibrational frequencies of consciousness in multiple dimensional ways, whatever those ways mean to you. You are not locked into a limited creative process. You are not bound by fears. Your Vision Center illuminates your unlimited creative potential. You are the only one who can enlighten and illuminate your life as you activate your Vision Center. You do not have to be in a meditative state or altered state of consciousness to see through your Vision Center.

Taurus, the bull, is the sign of strength in the physical realm. He represents the Second House in the Zodiac. Two numerically symbolizes the alignment of your physical strength with the strength of your Higher Consciousness of vision. What you see for yourself through your Higher Consciousness can never be negated or taken away from you. You are your vision. You are the source of your strength. Now you can see what you comprehend as your Truth. You can see it because your Vision Center reveals it to you.

Twelfth Chakra/Pituitary: Activation

The key to the activation of your Thirteen Chakras is established through the vibration of consciousness of the disciple Peter. He radiates the frequency of the faith consciousness. In his journey to his Higher Consciousness, Peter tested his faith. After Jesus' arrest, he denied knowing Him three times, later repenting his denial. Metaphorically, Peter did not trust his Higher Self, his Christed Consciousness, or God within him. When his faith was restored, he became a leader and spokesman of the disciples. The lesson is that faith is not something outside of yourself. It is found within you by trusting your Higher Consciousness, the God within you, and releasing the fears of your ego.

This faith consciousness signifies your receptivity and your permission to accept the Truth that God is within you and that you are God. God had never been outside of you. And your path to God does not require a mediator. The path to God IS inside of you. And God is not a gender.

God is a vibration of consciousness that resonates through your unconditional love and your faith. Unconditional love has no conditions. Faith is comprehending unconditional love in every cell of your body, on every level of your being. Unconditional love and faith are vibrational expressions of energy that do not hold a vibrational frequency of fear or opposition. The Godness energy within you begins to activate through your pituitary gland as you surrender the frequency of duality through unconditional love and faith.

The expression of oppositional energy, either individually or collectivity, only exists because it is held in the consciousness of the old worn-out Seven Chakras in your body. They have served their purpose. Now in the No-Time, No-Space within you, only you can choose to embrace the shift from the lower vibrational field of third dimensional fear consciousness to the vibrational frequency of the Godness Consciousness within you.

You have the knowledge, the experience and the faculties of the discipleships within you to create and manifest this shift. The shift is about creating your Heaven on Earth into your physical world, not just envisioning it up in the "etherics." You do have the right. It is your Inheritance to create your Heaven on Earth.

This is what raising your consciousness, expanding your vibration, and creating your life through the Frequency of the Godness within you is all about. Otherwise, why bother to come to this planet in the first place? So why wait until you die to experience a version of Heaven? Haven't you been there, done that before, in the reincarnation and karma programs? It is time to create your "Heaven on Earth" on Earth. So you are above, so you are below in alignment.

It is up to you to connect and inter-link to all the multiple dimensional levels of your consciousness. Here is your empowerment in faith and unconditional love, comprehending that you have it all inside you. You are all that you require, desire and deserve to be.

The First House in the astrological cycle is Aries. Aries, representing the number one metaphorically, is analogous to an idea originating from your creativity. In your higher vibrational frequency of consciousness, in the alignment of your multiple dimensional Self, you comprehend that you are not only the Creator, the creativity, and the creation, but you are the Originator of your idea.

Each new idea emanating from the passion of your Truth deserves to be manifested in your life. Each day is a new beginning in which is a space provided for you to bring your new ideas to fruition in your physical world. In this higher vibrational frequency of your creativity, you are not attached to it from a perspective of past or future. You are in the moment with your creative process.

This is the genesis process within you. Producing your creation into your world outside of you begins with one idea about yourself. Perhaps the idea is about something you desire to have for yourself, or an idea of a relationship you desire to have in your life. Whatever that idea is, it is founded upon consciousness.

When the consciousness is based upon fears, whether you are conscious of the fear or not, so is your idea. And what you produce into your physical world is birthed from a reality of fearfulness. The production of your idea will only be as clear of fear as you are. You really have a choice in your creative process. You can create your life with or without fear. This requires you to completely comprehend from which foundation your idea originates - from fear or from your Truth.

The whole purpose of ascending to your Higher Consciousness is recognizing that any and all ideas about yourself, about your life, about this world, about your path on this planet, have been based on fear at some level of your consciousness. Overcoming all of the old Fear Programs and how they have affected the idea of your relationships with yourself, your family, your friends, your foes, and what you have created outside of yourself, is your journey of raising your consciousness and letting go of the debilitating fears.

You can change your idea, keep the same idea, and even expand your idea. However, only after you make a choice that it is up to you to recognize that you have the empowerment within you to acknowledge and accept that God is within you, will you then accept that your ideas do not have to be based on a reality of fear.

This is what is known as co-creating your life with the essence and energy of the Godness within you. The basis of your idea, or multiplicity of ideas, begins to manifest from a higher vibrational frequency into a reality of living in your "Heaven on Earth," whatever your idea of your "Heaven on Earth" is. It is up to you.

Thirteenth Chakra/The Crown: Ascension/Unlimited

The Thirteenth Chakra represents the energy of your Christed Consciousness. Your Christed Consciousness is your ascension above and beyond the fear-based paradigm of duality. Jesus, in his physical death and resurrection, represents the shift in consciousness from the Duality Programs of fear to the vibration and frequency of unconditional love regardless of what is happening in the world "outside." He had emotionally detached from the programming and lived in his Christed Consciousness.

Your Christed Consciousness is your ascension above and beyond the emotions and the emotional attachments to the third dimensional programs. You have broken through the grid of recycled patterns, behaviors, and actions. Your grid is a new pattern of openness, expansion, and unlimited creativity.

As you have been activating this newer Chakra system, you have not only been letting go of the limitations of the third dimensional programs, you are now experiencing through your Feeling Center the energy field of consciousness that is unlimited. Your concepts about life are unlimited. Your creativity is unlimited. You are unlimited.

You can now ask yourself what it is you feel about your Truth and how you choose to define it. Always remember the Truth of yourself is not in opposition to your Higher Consciousness in any way. Your Truth is always compatible and in synchronicity with your Higher Consciousness. In your own personal life's evolution, it is your commitment to yourself to integrate all the levels of your consciousness. You do this so you can not only know and understand, but comprehend your Truth on all these levels of your Self. As One being, you are not a singularity. You are a multiple dimensional being of Oneness and so is your Truth.

In the stages of opening the energy vortices of the Thirteen Chakras, the point is to align your Higher Consciousness throughout your entire physical body, connecting, inter-linking and integrating all the levels of your consciousness in all the dimensions and realms in which you participate. You are consciously connected to your multiple dimensional Self.

Your Truth is multiple dimensional. Your creativity is multiple dimensional. Your life is multiple dimensional, and you comprehend that you are becoming One with your Self on your multiple dimensional levels of experiences and expressions of your Self. You are comprehending also that your Truth is as mutable and flexible as the Universal Consciousness of Oneness.

When you serve and honor yourself as One with the Godness energy within you, your Higher Consciousness, you honor and serve all who participate with you in your life. You make the choice for your participation, not just on this dimension, but on any other dimension in which you choose to interact. You can participate by choice because you are aware of the different levels of consciousness.

Numerically, thirteen equals a four. Four is the dimension of the No-Time and No Space of your Now. Living in the Now is no longer affected by your past or past/future. The past is only a resource of information to use or discard and has no substance to re-create a future based on the past that does not serve you.

You have many futures to create from your Now. You are not limited in timelines of linear time. Now you have the potential to create limitless futures, not just one singular future. You will have many future moments in which to use your unlimited abilities to create. What you create is up to you.

In your Becoming you are remembering that you are consciousness and everything about you is consciousness. Aligning and balancing all the multiple dimensional levels of your consciousness within your physical body in the Now is becoming aware and accepting consciously...Who You Are.

What's next? The Fourteenth through the Nineteenth Chakras. Stay tuned and be in alignment with your Self. You deserve it.

Note: Not only do you have the assistance from the other dimensions and realms for guidance, the new children that are being birthed on this planet from the year 2002 going forward are beyond the frequency and vibration of the Indigo children. These children are called, the Double Heart children. Their consciousness is already at the higher vibrational frequencies that support this shift of consciousness for the people living on this planet. Because these children carry this Higher Consciousness, they will not have the challenges of the Indigo children. They will not be as affected by the lower fear-based consciousness. They know at their surface consciousness Who They Are. They are here to support us in remembering Who We Are.

CHAKRA	ZODIAC	DISCIPLE	BODY	ENERGY	ESSENTIAL OIL	CRYSTAL
13	Transcension	God Within	Unlimited	Christ Consciousness	Myrrh	Azeztulite
12	Aries 1st House	Peter	Pituitary	Activation	Tuberose	Charoite
11	Taurus 2nd House	Andrew	Third Eye	Vision Center	Frankincense	Tanzanite
10	Gemini 3rd House	Philip	Throat	Communication	Yarrow	Celestite
9	Cancer 4th House	James	Nervous System	Conscious Integration	Basil Nepal	Amethyst
8	Leo 5th House	John	Heart	Feeling Center	Rose Moroccan	Emerald
7	Virgo 6th House	Nathanael Bartholomew	Diaphragm	Information Assimiilation	Eucalysus Radiata	Yellow Flourite
6	Libra 7th House	James	Solar Plexus	Balance and Understanding	Boronia	Citrine
5	Scorpio 8th House	Matthew	Reproductive Organs	Creativity	Jasmine	Carnelian
4	Sagittarius 9th House	Thomas	Hips and Upper Legs	Passion and Commitment	Vetyver	Sunstone (natural)
3	Capricorn 10th House	Simon	Knees	What You Stand For	Patchouli	Danburite
2	Aquarius 11th House	Thaddaeus	Ankles	Female/Male Energy Alignment	Helichrysum	Kunzite
1	Pisces 12th House	Judas	Feet	Soul of Your Earth Body Foundation	Spikenard	Rhodocrosite

The Inheritance: The New Thirteen Galactic Human Chakra System

Your transcended physical body of the One Consciousness of Multidimensional Being, completely integrated and aligned in your new field of Electro-Magnetic Energy, lifes through the Divine Law of your Discipleship of Unconditional Love for instant manifestation of your creative seed/idea.

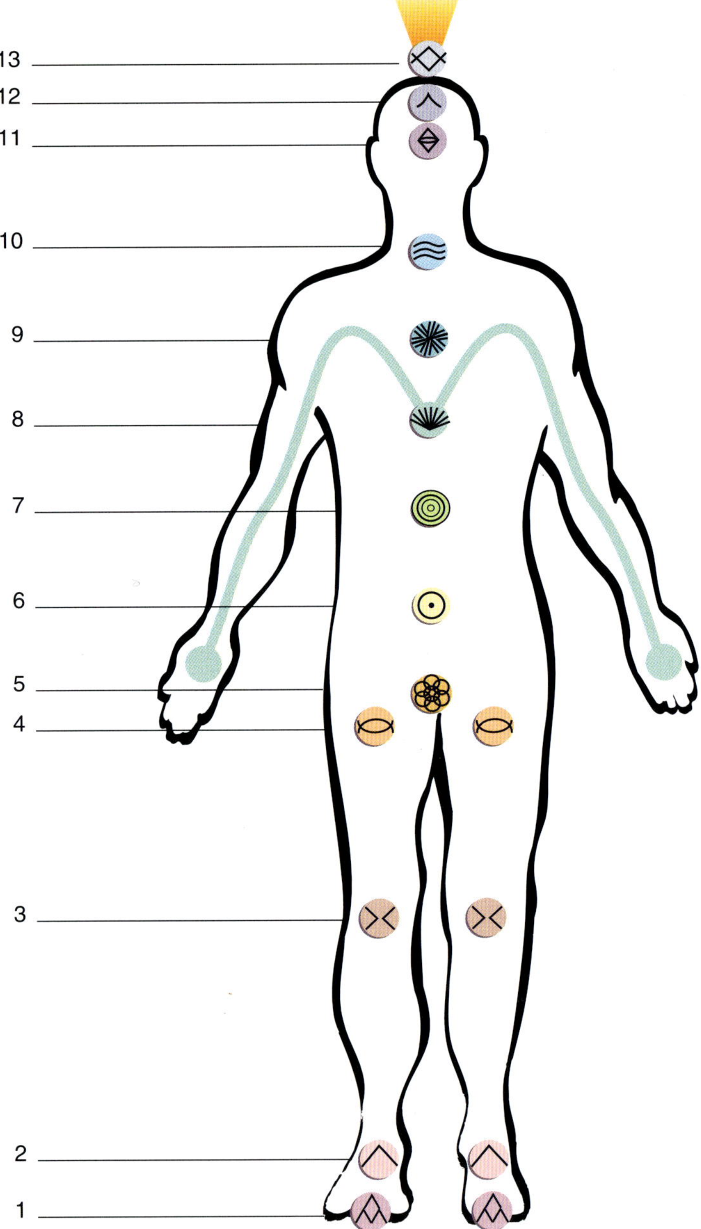

The Shift in Polarity in Your Electromagnetic Field: A Unified Field of Consciousness

The Thirteen Chakras: Their Colors and Symbols

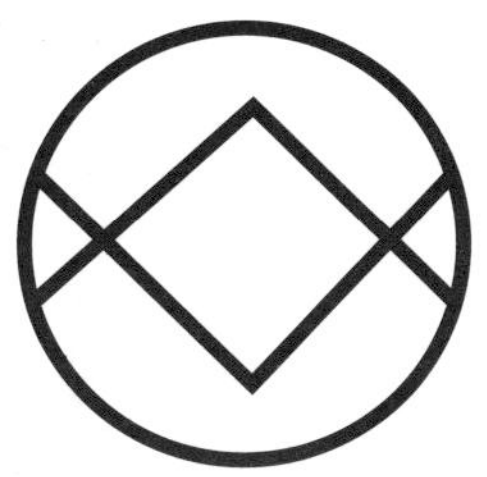

Chapter 8
Your Discs Of Knowledge, Your Akashic Records
Accessing Your Records, Your History, Your Self

I release all fears. I now trust the process of life.
I know that life is for me. I stand straight and tall with love.

Louise L. Hay
Heal Your Body

A unique and incredible methodology in your healing journey is to access the information that is stored throughout the cells of your body, as has been stated previously. In the process of accessing the information, emotional releases will occur.

Through the releasing of your emotional issues at your cellular level to access the vital information about your history, you also have an optional course to obtain information about yourself from your time continuum. This alternative methodology is usually not as emotionally charged. Through this information, you will have the ability to more clearly define and select the information that you require to keep for this lifetime or to delete it as no longer valuable to you. This resource is a wealth of information and is not as emotionally challenging to release.

This information is stored within your own personal Akashic library of records. This library of information is stored or encoded in each of the discs in your spinal column. The purpose of each disc is to store all the information about your lifetimes and all of the experiences within those lifetimes, your time continuum. Each of your lifetimes has many purposes, just as this one does. Now you have the opportunity to access not only your purposes, but what you have learned or not learned from those lifetimes. Accessing your personal Akashic library supports you in remembering Who You Are, what you have been, how you experienced the consciousness of a particular lifetime, and what you can now bring to your present lifetime from these experiences and purposes.

As has been discussed before, there is nothing outside of you that has been created into the physical world until it has been created or invented from within you. Your creativity is also influenced by the collective consciousness in which you participated. Simply said, *from the inside manifests the outside*. Whether you are the actual manifestor of an idea produced into a product is not the issue. When an idea of the product is manifested or manufactured into the physical in a certain frame of linear time and you are living in that time frame, you are choosing to be of that consciousness, whether the inventor or the user. Your co-participation is part of the consciousness, whether you agree with it, like it or not.

At this particular time, the utilization of CD's and CDI technologies are the "outside" manufactured representations of your internal informational discs. The "compacted discs" hold incredible amounts of written and graphic information, and in this linear time are now available to the masses around the world. Correspondingly so, you now have access in this linear time to your own personal Akashic library stored on your discs.

There are various ways to access the information. You can focus your consciousness and energy into a particular disc in your spinal column. With the assistance of a Quantum Energy Therapist, you can retrieve the information, just as you would from a disc that you insert into your computer. By placing crystals on various areas of your spinal column, they can be used as conductors of energy to release information stored on your discs. It is the same process. However, the frequency and vibration of the crystals act as conduits that sometimes make accessing the information easier.

Whatever method you choose, accessing your Akashic records

will assist you in recalling, retrieving, recollecting and remembering your past. Doing this supports you in clearing and healing your present time, and will assist you to create your future based on information that serves you now without repeating the old, unconscious patterns and behaviors.

Depending upon your choice of action in your healing and clearing journey in this lifetime, you may consider clearing the emotional issues that are held within your physical body now, and then proceed to access the All Information and All Time of you recorded on your discs in your Akashic library.

You and only you can determine the difficulty or the ease of your healing process. Beyond your ego's expectations of the difficulty or ease, in your consciousness lies the Is-ness of the experience. In the Is-ness there is no challenge or difficulty. It just Is. Remember, it is your ego that is expecting the challenge. In the healing process, your body intuitively knows exactly what to do and how to do it. Your body knows what is required to be released at that moment, at your level of your consciousness. Trust your intuition and your body. Do not trust your ego.

Your commitment, unconditionally, without any judgment to healing yourself is a physical, spiritual, emotional, and soul requirement to move through and beyond duality's oppositional energy of consciousness. Whatever your expectations of the process of healing are, whether easy or difficult, it is up to you to make that choice. It will only be as challenging as you make it.

After a release the body feels lighter. The reason for this is the body has released the emotional attachment to an issue. Now it is also released from the physical density of the old consciousness attached to the issue. And, though it may feel lighter, the body normally requires a period of time to recoup its energy from the release of the emotional experience.

These releases may come in the form of sounds or tones. These are vibrations and frequencies that are being released in order to access the information. The releasing from your discs is not usually as emotional as the releasing of cellular memory, memorization, and sound from your body.

Your Throat Chakra is a vital key to releasing your sounds and tones from your body. This Chakra allows your body the physical releasing of these sounds and tones. This is important because your sounds and tones are inter-linked with the areas of your body that are releasing your emotional issues. Each area of your body has its own memory or memorization of a particular sound connected to the emotional issue and the release. Your Throat Chakra gives voice and sound to your releasing, whether emotional issues or historical information.

Through sleep and meditation the body regenerates its energy in this new expanded state of consciousness. The physical body requires this time for regeneration and renewal. Coming into balance with this newer, expanded awareness is also integral for the body to process both physically and consciously.

As you consciously access your knowledge, you free yourself from the density of oppositional consciousness. You comprehend that the opposition, regardless of your lifetime, was always inside of you. Because oppositional consciousness is inside of you and everyone else, opposition must manifest on the outside. What you delete of the programming within you, whether in your cellular body or on your discs, no longer exists outside in your world. Whether the programming exists for someone else is not your issue or problem. You have detached.

The faster and more deliberately everyone detaches from the programs, the more the programs are released from the collective consciousness. What no longer exists in the collective consciousness, no longer exists.

Your entire body of consciousness, physical, spiritual, emotional, cellular, and within your soul, your Chakras, your aura, and everything within you, are your multiple dimensional levels of your consciousness, your being-ness and your essence of life. What, where, and how you focus your consciousness is your life.

So you Are.